MAN CAVES

MAN CAVES

HOW TO CREATE THE ULTIMATE
MALE SANCTUARY

DOMINIC BLISS

DOG 'n' BONE

Published in 2017 by Dog 'n' Bone Books
An imprint of Ryland Peters & Small Ltd
20–21 Jockey's Fields   341 E 116th St
London WC1R 4BW   New York, NY 10029

www.rylandpeters.com

10 9 8 7 6 5 4 3 2 1

A CIP catalog record for this book is available from
the Library of Congress and the British Library.

ISBN: 978 1 911026 14 3

Printed in China

Designer: Eoghan O'Brien
Illustrator: John Riordan
Editor: Pete Jorgensen

Note: currency conversions were calculated
in November 2016 and rates will fluctuate
between then and the date of publication.

CONTENTS

INTRODUCTION

Every man needs a man cave—
a sanctuary he can escape to where
women and children are banned,
booze flows freely, and sport is
always on the television. A warm,
cozy refuge where he and his fellow
cavemen can indulge their hobbies
to their hearts' content.

Man caves might be located in the
attic, the spare room, the basement,
even at the bottom of the garden.
As long as these spaces allow you to
kick back and relax from the stress
of domestic life and nagging family
members, then their location isn't
important. Simply having one is the
most crucial thing.

In this book, we suggest 27 different
themes for your man cave, with
practical advice on the décor, the
gadgets, and the information you
need to transform your space into
the ultimate male retreat. There
are tips on all sorts of crucial life

skills you're going to need inside your man cave: how to store wine, mix cocktails, taste beer, collect comics and vinyl records, observe the stars, survive nuclear fallout, keep pets, and sharpen knives. You'll learn how to set up the perfect home office, display animal trophies, build a dance floor and a golf putting green, take photographs, and ensure your bikes are thief-proof. You'll discover the world's most amazing gym equipment, train sets, power tools, coffee, cigar humidors, sports memorabilia, and vintage video games. All life is here... Ready for pride of place in your man cave.

Whether you're planning a brand-new man cave, or you want to pimp your existing room, in this book you will discover all the answers.

ENTER THE MAN CAVES...

HOME GYM

Fitness junkies need a home gym where they can sweat, grunt, and kiss their guns while admiring themselves in the mirror. It's often an activity done alone, but workout buddies will keep you motivated and spot you while you bench 175 pounds (80 kilograms) on the pec deck.

Ambient temperature is crucial in a home gym. In summer, air conditioning or fans will be required. In winter, heating needs only to be minimal—if you get hot, you're not working out hard enough.

Space is at a premium in most man caves, so be prudent about which large machines you choose. It's good to have one cardio machine (perhaps a spin bike?), but if you want to get properly aerobic, you can always head outside; or increase the intensity of your exercises.

There are two species of gym users. The first errs toward aerobic workouts and is leaner. The second concentrates on lifting weights and is beefier. Both species obsess over their diets—aerobic junkies keep the calories limited and weights junkies bulk up with extra protein shakes. From morning to night they wear sports clothing that accentuates their finest features and reveals impressive muscle groups. Tattoos and closely cropped haircuts are popular, as is steroid abuse... Allegedly. When a fitness junkie gets into the stride of his workout you can spot the temporal arteries pulsating angrily on the side of his forehead.

GYM ENTERTAINMENT

Don't underestimate the importance of a top-notch stereo and TV for your home gym. Position the TV screen where it's easily visible from your cardio machine, and install quality speakers that link to both TV and sound system.

THE SET UP

- Kettlebells, barbells, and dumbbells
- Bench and rack
- Punchbag
- Fan or air-conditioning unit
- Big mirror
- Loud stereo
- Exercise mat
- Clock

ADVANTAGES OF A HOME GYM

1 It's always open.

2 It's downstairs/upstairs/out the back, so there are no excuses not to work out.

3 You don't have to wait to use the equipment or weights. Get straight in there.

4 The only sweat on the equipment is your own.

5 You can grunt/ roar/ scream to your heart's content. (This isn't permitted in some commercial gyms where they install a "lunk alarm" that goes off if you work out too vigorously.)

6 You can wear the tightest or skimpiest workout clothing you like. Pec flys in your Y-fronts? Why not?

7 You choose the music. Girlie pop does not a buff body create.

MOTIVATIONAL DÉCOR

Every gym needs a large mirror to work out in front of. Yes, it's vain, but if you can see your muscles bulging as you smash your guns, it will encourage you to keep going.

Hang posters of various gym heroes on the wall of your man cave. These may include Arnie, Charles Atlas, Bruce Lee, "Stone Cold" Steve Austin, and a skinned cartoon human with all his muscles captioned. There's just one rule: these posters may NOT include Jane Fonda, Mr Motivator, Richard Simmons, or The Green Goddess.

KEEP COOL

Hot summers in your neck of the woods? Then you're going to need to install a proper air-conditioning system. Opt for something that isn't so noisy that it drowns out your motivational tunes on the stereo. For fitness junkies in more northern climes, a fan will suffice. Make it a portable tower fan (desk fans aren't nearly powerful enough), so that you can position it to blow directly onto your body, wherever you happen to be working out.

Bladeless fans are great as there's no risk you'll catch headphone leads in the fan mid sit-up.

DRINKS DISPENSER

You're going to get hot. You're going to get thirsty. You either need a water cooler or a mini fridge. The latter is often better since you can keep cool energy and protein drinks as well as water in it. Plus snacks, of course.

STRONG FLOOR

Over the years, your body and your weights are going to be slamming down onto your man cave floor thousands of times. For that reason it needs to have a sturdy floor base. On top you can place interlocking foam mats that absorb the impact and sound of dropped weights. They are also easy to wipe clean of sweat.

TOP WORKOUT TUNES

For lifting weights:

- *Enter Sandman* by Metallica
- *Back in Black* by AC/DC
- *Pump Up The Jam* by Technotronic
- *Push It* by Salt-N-Pepa
- *No One Knows* by Queens of the Stone Age

For punchbag or skipping rope:

- *Eye of the Tiger* by Survivor
- *Mama Said Knock You Out* by LL Cool J
- *Harder, Better, Faster, Stronger* by Daft Punk

For the treadmill:

- *Born to Run* by Bruce Springsteen
- *Keep on Running* by The Spencer Davis Group

For the spin bike:

- *Tour de France* by Kraftwerk
- *The Bike Song* by Mark Ronson
- *Freewheel Burning* by Judas Priest

ESSENTIAL EQUIPMENT

PUNCHBAG

The focal point of your home gym should be a heavy-duty punchbag, hanging proudly in the center of the room. This is where you will vent the majority of your pent-up aggression, so make sure it's made from leather with strong stitching, D-rings, and chains.

Karl Lagerfeld once designed a limited-edition punchbag for Louis Vuitton. Priced at around $175,000 (£140,000), it was adorned with the brand's famous brown-and-gold monogram print, and came with a solid storage trunk, stand, mat, and matching boxing gloves. Exactly what every dictator needs to practice beating his enemies on.

BARBELL AND PLATE SET

You can exercise pretty much every major muscle group with this piece of equipment: squats, lunges, deadlifts, cleans, presses, curls. Opt for the larger Olympic bar, which can accommodate heavier weights when you get really serious.

ADJUSTABLE BENCH

In a full-size gym you'd have all sorts of benches for all sorts of exercises, but in your man cave, space is at a premium. Get an adjustable bench that can be angled according to your workout requirements.

RACK

This will take up a lot of room in your home gym, but it's important because you'll rarely have a workout buddy to spot you. A rack allows you to rack the barbell safely. A full-size rack can also be used for chin-ups and pull-ups.

REAL-LIFE HOME GYM

Some guys need a lot of weights. Actor Mark Wahlberg needs so many that, at his former 11,500-square foot (3,500-square meter) home in Beverly Hills, he converted an old airport hangar into his home gym. It included a boxing ring and weights as far as the eye could see, plus a mezzanine area for the cardio machines. Outside was a basketball court and a swimming pool. Of course.

MOTIVATIONAL QUOTES

Bare walls won't inspire you to work out. What you need are motivational quotes writ in letters large and bold.

Sweat is just your fat crying.

Go hard or go home!

EAT BIG! LIFT BIG! GET BIG!

SQUAT TILL YOU PUKE.

Winners train, losers complain.

If the bar ain't bending, you're just pretending.

PAIN IS JUST WEAKNESS LEAVING THE BODY.

I got 99 problems, but a bench ain't one.

ADJUSTABLE DUMBBELLS

It's unlikely you'll have room for a whole set of different dumbbells. One solution is adjustable dumbbells, which usually accommodate up to 50 pounds (25 kilograms) at least.

EXERCISE MAT

Sweat, blood, tears... This has got to be of the wipe-clean variety.

GYM CLOCK

Make sure it has a second hand (great for timing yourself) and it's large enough to see from the other side of your man cave when viewed through sweat-soaked eyes.

KETTLEBELLS

Every self-respecting gym needs a set of kettlebells. Favored by the likes of Navy Seals, SWAT teams, Sylvester Stallone, and (in times past) the Soviet Red Army, kettlebell lifting combines strength, flexibility, and aerobics into one almighty workout.

"The kettlebell is the AK-47 of physical training hardware," says Pavel Tsatsouline, former Soviet Union special forces trainer. "It's a cannonball with a handle! Simple, sinister, brutal, and ferociously effective for developing explosive strength, dramatic power, and never-say-die conditioning. Guaranteed to forge a rugged, resilient, densely muscled frame. Built to withstand the hardest beating and dish it right back out, 24/7!"

OTHER ESSENTIALS

- Medicine ball
- Resistance bands
- Wooden plyo box
- Skipping rope
- Suspension training kit

There's only one place for an oenophile's man cave and that's in the cellar, of course. Anywhere else and your 1982 Château Lafite Rothschild just won't lay down properly. You require coolness, darkness, and humidity to ensure your wine improves rather than deteriorates with age.

Alongside your multiple racks of wine you should have a very comfortable tasting area, complete with sink, miniature bar, fridge, and all the various drinking paraphernalia, including a spittoon. Not that you'll be doing much spitting—this man cave will stock only the finest vintages available to humanity. It would be criminal to waste them.

Most wine buffs tend to have a certain look, involving red chinos, striped shirt, blue blazer, and a big nose. They're not all total idiots, however. In recent years, the appreciation of fine wine has become greatly democratized.

WINE CELLAR

THE SET UP

- Wine racks
- Sink
- Bar
- Fridge
- Glasses
- Decanters
- Ice buckets
- Bar-mounted corkscrews
- Spittoon

SIZE MATTERS

One way to blag it as a wine buff is to know the different names for the different bottle sizes. Aim to have an example of each in your man cave.

- Piccolo (0.1875 liters)
- Quarter (0.2 liters)
- Chopine (0.25 liters)
- Demi (0.375 liters)
- Jennie (0.5 liters)
- Clavelin (0.62 liters)
- Standard bottle (0.75 liters)
- Magnum (1.5 liters)
- Marie Jeanne (2.25 liters)
- Jeroboam (3 liters)
- Rehoboam (4.5 liters)
- McKenzie (5 liters)
- Imperial or Methuselah (6 liters)
- Salmanazar (9 liters)
- Balthazar (12 liters)
- Nebuchadnezzar (15 liters)
- Melchior or Solomon (18 liters)
- Sovereign (26.25 liters)
- Primat or Goliath (27 liters)
- Melchizedek or Midas (30 liters)

SABRAGE

A wine man cave deserves some serious ostentation. What could be more ostentatious than sabrage? For the uninitiated, this is a Champagne-bottle-opening ceremony using a saber. Basically, you hold the bottle at an angle, cork facing away from you, saber resting on its neck. Next, slide the blunt edge of the saber firmly and smoothly along the seam that runs along the length of the neck, decapitating the entire head of the bottle—collar, cork, cage, and all.

Apparently, it's a ceremony that dates back to the time of Napoleon, when the hussars of his light cavalry used to open bottles with their sabers (or swords), while mounted and at a gallop. Nowadays, it's a trick that requires both practice and sobriety. Careless party hosts have been known to inadvertently part company with their thumbs.

King of sabrage is an American called Ashrita Furman who, in 2015, sliced the top off 66 Champagne bottles within the space of one minute, earning himself a worthy Guinness World Record.

Your man cave may not be the biggest of spaces. Even if you can't swing a cat in it, make sure you can at least swing a saber.

REAL-LIFE WINE CELLAR

Scottish folk-rocker Al Stewart (most famous for his 1976 hit, *The Year of the Cat*) has a personal collection of 1,800 bottles in wine cabinets in his San Francisco home. He's constantly on the lookout for new vintages and admits he spends half of all his disposable income on wine.

"At any given time, there are 40 to 50 wines waiting for me to taste," he told *Decanter* magazine. "It's obsessive behavior, but at least I know I'm not alone."

In 2000, Stewart released an album dedicated to his own collection called *Down in the Cellar*. Tracks included *Waiting for Margaux*, *Tasting History*, *Under a Wine-Stained Moon*, and *The Shiraz Shuffle*.

WINE BUCKET LIST

Here's a Champagne bucket that should be on every wine buff's bucket list. From Dutch designer Van Perckens, the Nr. 8 cooler is made from 15 pounds (7 kilograms) of 20-carat gold and priced at almost $750,000 (£600,000). It comes in a rosewood case with six Champagne goblets and a pair of tailored serving gloves. At this price it just wouldn't do to smudge the glasses.

HOW TO START A FINE-WINE COLLECTION

Even if your wine collection fails to turn hedge-fund managers green with envy, there are still certain tricks you can employ to maintain its worth—both to you and to potential buyers, should you sell it on.

PLAN Don't buy wines haphazardly. Plan which wines you want to collect and stick to them.

BUY WHAT YOU LOVE Then, if you never sell it, at least you can enjoy it.

NOTES Keep detailed notes on all the bottles in your collection. Include the producer, the year, the name, the grape, etc. If you drink it, tick it off your list and add some tasting notes.

DOCUMENTATION Every time you buy a bottle, save the receipt, the auction notes, the delivery details, the business card of the vendor, etc.

PACKAGING Keep the original wine cases or boxes intact as proof of provenance.

VALUATION Have your collection regularly valued, especially if it's an expensive one. It's useful info if you plan to sell, or for insurance purposes.

GET SOMEONE ELSE TO DO IT If all the above sounds a bit too much like hard work, why not seek out some professional help? These days, respected wine merchants offer monthly investment plans where you pay them a specific amount every month and they take care of the rest.

HOW TO STORE WINE

OK, so your wine man cave isn't quite a stone cellar deep beneath a 16th-century Bordeaux château. Still, that doesn't stop you following a few simple guidelines to protect your wine when you store it.

KEEP IT FLAT (OR FLAT-ISH)

Wine is traditionally stored horizontally. This is so the liquid keeps the cork damp and stops it drying out. If it dries out, there's a risk that air could seep in and spoil the wine. This can't happen with screw-capped bottles, so you can store them at any angle you like.

Some collectors prefer to keep their wine horizontal, but with the neck angled very slightly upward. You can do this by propping up the front of your wine rack with a wedge. This allows both the liquid and the air bubble inside the bottle to make contact with the cork. The liquid keeps the cork damp and stops it drying out while, should temperature fluctuations occur, it will be air rather than wine that is forced out through the cork. All very complicated, but it's sure to impress your fellow wine buffs.

KEEP IT COOL

The ideal temperature for wine storage is 50–59°F (10–15°C). The lightest wines can freeze at 25°F (-4°C), forcing the corks out of the necks, while at 85°F (30°C) and above, wines can be irreparably damaged. Try to maintain a fairly constant temperature in your cave. Large fluctuations can cause the wine to expand and contract rapidly,

THE ULTIMATE WINE COLLECTION

If money was no object, which bottles would grace your collection? Here is a list of some of the most expensive wines ever sold.

Romanée-Conti DRC 1990

$28,112 (£22,600)

You need three grape vines to make a bottle of this delicious Pinot Noir. In 1996, a set of eight sold for nearly $250,000 (£200,000).

Penfolds Grange Hermitage 1951

$38,420 (£30,850)

Experts reckon there are only 20 bottles of this gorgeous Australian red left in existence. It sold at auction in 2004.

Massandra 1775 sherry

$43,500 (£35,000)

Russia's Massandra winery stores some very old sherry indeed. In 2001, its oldest bottle of all was sold at auction.

Château d'Yquem 1787

$100,000 (£80,000)

1787 spawned a vintage white wine that sold for a cool hundred grand in 2006.

Château Mouton Rothschild 1945

$114,614 (£92,000)

The final year of World War 2 was a vintage one for Bordeaux wines, especially this, a jeroboam of which sold at auction in 1997.

Cheval Blanc 1947

$135,125 (£108,500)

A three-liter bottle of this Merlot was purchased in San Francisco in 2006.

Château Lafite 1787

$156,450 (£125,650)

A bottle of this was bought in 1985. Etched on the glass were the initials ThJ, which led some to believe it once belonged to President Thomas Jefferson. Others aren't so sure.

with the risk of air seeping in. Hang a thermometer near your wine so you can monitor the air temperature.

KEEP IT DARK Why do many wines come in dark glass bottles? This is because sunlight damages wine and affects the taste. Position bottles where they won't be exposed to sunlight.

KEEP IT QUITE HUMID Keep the wine too dry for several years, and there's a risk the corks will dry out, allowing air to seep in and damage the wine. That said, rooms that are too humid can damage the bottle labels and make the wine difficult to re-sell.

KEEP IT STILL Too much vibration in your cave can stop sediment in older wines from settling. Worth knowing if you live in an earthquake zone.

Château Margaux 1787
$225,000 (£180,750)
In 1989, the New York wine merchant who owned this bottle took it to a special dinner. What wasn't so special, however, was the service, since the waiter accidentally knocked it to the floor. Insurers coughed up to the tune of $225,000.

Heidsieck 1907
$275,000 (£221,000)
During World War 1, a German submarine torpedoed a boat stocked with bottles of Heidsieck Champagne destined for the court of Tsar Nicholas II of Russia. Eighty years later, its cargo was salvaged and sold at various auctions.

Screaming Eagle Cabernet 1992
$500,000 (£400,000)
Granted, it was sold for charity at an auction in 2000, so the price was artificially raised. However, an imperial bottle of this Californian Cabernet holds the record for the highest price ever paid for a single bottle of wine.

PROFESSIONAL STORAGE

If you're lucky enough to own some seriously good wine, you might want to invest in a proper wine cabinet. As well as keeping the bottles at the perfect storage temperature, a cabinet maintains the humidity and sometimes features dampeners to reduce vibration.

Why not go the whole hog and install an actual wine cellar beneath your man cave? One of the most impressive available is a spiral cellar. It's cylindrical in shape, dug into the floor, and stores the wine bottles on shelves that encircle a central spiral staircase, all encased by a trapdoor. The downside is your man cave obviously has to be on the ground floor to accommodate it. The upside is that it looks like the kind of place a Bond villain would store his precious wine.

There are several installers who offer spiral wine cellars, including Genuwine Cellars in the USA and Canada, Spiral Cellars in the UK and Australia, Wine and Wood Ltd in New Zealand, and Helicave across continental Europe.

Professional mixologists like to portray their job as some sort of dark art, far beyond the capabilities of us mere mortals. That's a load of bull—anyone can be a great cocktail maker. All you need is a man cave and a well-stocked bar.

The focus of any bar is the bar top. Choose a surface that is both beautiful and hardwearing. Behind the bar, or against the wall, you need a work counter and a small sink at a level lower than the bar top. This is where you'll be creating your drinks. Under the bar should be a speed rail where the basic spirits are kept. Above the back wall is where to put the good stuff—with plenty of interesting bottles on display. You'll also need an ample fridge freezer with a glass door and masses of ice. Finally, choose some cool bar stools, comfortable enough that you can park your backside on them all night while slowly getting nicely sozzled.

COCKTAIL BAR

The following drinks and ingredients are more than enough for a killer cocktail bar. However, don't waste valuable drinking time worrying if you don't stock all of them.

SPIRITS Vodka, London dry gin, white rum, dark rum, tequila, bourbon, Scotch whisky, Cognac.

LIQUEURS Orange liqueur, maraschino liqueur, coffee liqueur, crème de cassis, crème de cacao.

VERMOUTHS AND BITTERS
Dry vermouth, sweet red vermouth, Campari, Angostura and orange bitters.

MIXERS ETC Sugar syrup, Tabasco, grenadine, fruit juices, soda water, tonic water, cola, ginger ale, cherries, oranges, mint leaves, sugar, salt, and pepper.

ICE So much ice.

LEMON JUICE AND LIME JUICE
Lots of it.

BAR TOP

This is where you'll be creating and drinking the tastiest cocktails known to man, so it's worth splashing out on a beautiful bar top. No Formica here, please. There's going to be spillage, slammed glasses, snacks, smoking. You need a surface that is both aesthetic and hardwearing. Think granite, slate, teak, cherry wood, oak, resin, quartz composite, or copper.

The standard height for a drinking bar top is 42 inches (107 centimeters), with an overhang of 12–14 inches (30–35 centimeters). On the mixing side of the bar, or against the back wall, you'll need a lower-level counter to prepare drinks on—around 36-inches (90-centimeters) high.

DON'T COCK UP YOUR COCKTAILS

If you want to impress your man-cave guests with adventurous drinks, you'll need to hone your mixing skills.

One man with a unique set of skills is Scottish cocktail barman Mal Spence, who, for the 2014 Commonwealth Games, created a mix of no less than 71 ingredients, which, like the competitors at the games, hailed from Commonwealth nations all over the planet. They included prickly pear from Namibia, cashew nut from Sierra Leone, dragon fruit from Belize, saffron from Pakistan, durian from Brunei, okra from Jamaica, star anise from Malta, and avocado from Tonga. (Feeling queasy yet?) It was called The Commonwealth and could well be the most complicated cocktail ever created.

THE SET UP

- Bar top
- Bar stools
- Measuring cup/jigger
- Sink
- Fridge
- Glasses
- Bottles of spirits
- Ice bucket
- Cocktail shaker
- Strainer
- Corkscrew, swizzle sticks, napkins, etc.

GLASSWARE

You can really go to town here, spending a fortune on crystal glasses, but, equally, Ikea glasses, or similar, work just as well. These four styles will cover almost all bases.

ROCKS For short, strong drinks, usually on ice. Think a Negroni, Old Fashioned, or Whiskey Sour.

COCKTAIL AKA the Martini glass. Perfect for drinks served "straight up" with no ice, like (you guessed it) a Martini, Daiquiri, or Cosmopolitan.

HIGHBALL For refreshing long drinks, including the Mojito and Bloody Mary.

WINE GLASS Old faithful; as well as wine these are ideal for creamy Flips and after-dinner cocktails.

PREMIUM QUALITY

A good bar doesn't have to be solely about cocktails. If you really want to show off, try to get your hands on some super-expensive spirits. These special editions are among the highest-priced ever.

Angostura Legacy rum
$25,000 (£20,000)
Released to celebrate the 50th anniversary of Trinidad and Tobago's independence, this came with a crystal and silver decanter, and a silver stopper, wrapped up in a silk, velvet, and leather box.

Bowmore 1957 Scotch whisky
$165,000 (£132,000)
Housed in a glass and platinum bottle, this Islay malt whisky spent 43 years aging in a sherry cask, and a further 11 in a bourbon cask. Only 12 bottles were made.

Remy Martin Black Pearl Louis XIII Cognac
$165,000 (£132,000)
The eau de vie in this beautiful cognac matured for between 40 and 100 years. The Baccarat-designed bottle is hand-blown from black crystal.

Johnnie Walker Diamond Jubilee Scotch whisky
$165,000 (£132,000)
Released in 2012 to celebrate the Queen's 60th year on the throne, this Scotch was matured for 60 years. Sixty bottles were made and The Queen was given one. Prince Philip quaffed the lot. Probably.

The Dalmore 62 Scotch whisky
$200,000 (£160,000)
When it went on sale at Singapore's Changi airport, this was the world's most expensive whisky. Only 12 bottles were released.

Royal Salute Tribute to Honour Scotch whisky
$200,000 (£160,000)
Released in tribute to some very famous Scottish royal jewels (the Honours of Scotland), this Scotch came in a bottle adorned with silver, gold, and 413 diamonds. Not one to swig nonchalantly from.

Mendis coconut brandy
$1 million (£800,000)
This was distilled from coconut and matured in wooden casks. For some bizarre reason, the first edition sold for $1 million. You distil coconuts, you get monkeys.

Diva Vodka
$1 million (£800,000)
Yes, the vodka inside is very nice indeed, but you're mainly paying for the crystals and gemstones adorning the bottle.

Henry IV Dudognon Heritage Cognac Grande Champagne
$2 million (£1.6 million)
You'll squeeze only 1 liter of cognac out of this bottle, but you'll know that it's been aged for more than a century. And you'll be dazzled by the 6,500 diamonds, plus the gold and platinum bottle.

Ley .925 Tequila Pasion Azteca Ultra Premium Añejo
$3.5 million (£2.8 million)
Gold, platinum, lots of diamonds; you get the message. Alternatively, for this price you could buy Mexico's entire agave-plant crop and thereby corner the market.

NIGHTCLUB

Surely you're too old to be hanging out in nightclubs? Besides, what with overpriced drinks, rude bouncers, and the battle for an Uber-ride home, the whole experience just isn't suited to a self-respecting man of a certain age. Much better to build your own personal nightclub at home.

The first thing about this man cave nightspot is that it needs to be soundproofed. If you're partying away until the wee hours, you don't want irate neighbors calling the police in the middle of your set.

The focus of the club should be the DJ booth where you'll be spinning the finest tunes. This must be backed up with a professional-level sound system. Then think about the dance floor—a sprung wooden surface is normally best. What about a stage with a pole for those special dances? A small bar is required since nobody past a certain age dances unless inebriated. Finally, topping it all, you'll need a ceiling-mounted mirror ball and a few lights.

THE SET UP

- Sound system
- DJ booth
- Mirrorball and lighting
- Stage with pole
- Dance floor
- Bar

VITAL DJ EQUIPMENT

Yes, nowadays laptop DJs are ten a penny and you can mix with just a smart-phone app, but where's the soul in that? If you're going to have a nightclub in your man cave, surely you want to be spinning real discs on real turntables? Here's what you need. (See page 56 for ideas on amazing speaker systems.)

- Two DJ turntables
- Two DJ phono cartridges
- Two slipmats
- DJ mixer
- DJ headphones (these must look and sound the business—see page 30)
- RCA cable (don't mess around—get gold-plated)
- Speakers
- A record collection

HEADPHONE HEAVEN

You may be the most feckless DJ on the planet, with an ability to butcher songs not seen since Nickelback released a new album. Splash out on bank-shatteringly expensive headphones, however, and at least you'll look like a superstar DJ.

Ultrasone Edition 5
$2,749 (£1,600)
As well as the astounding quality, there's the Ethiopian long-haired sheep leather and the bog oak ear cups with a "seven-layer varnishing process."

Abyss AB-1266
$5,495 (£4,000)
An aluminum and steel body, plus lambskin pads make these arguably the most beautiful cans on the planet. Some experts even claim they produce the best sound on the planet.

NEEDLE ON THE RECORD

The Technics SL-1200 has been the industry standard for over 30 years, but what needles should be used with such an esteemed turntable? Consider buying these bad boys only if your DJing is really up to scratch. That said, don't you dare scratch with them. These are three of the most ridiculously expensive phono cartridges out there.

Clearaudio Goldfinger Statement phono cartridge
$15,000 (£10,000)
24-carat gold coil material, 14-carat gold cartridge body, and a boron cantilever. This is what dictators use to play their marching-into-battle music on.

Koetsu Coralstone platinum phono cartridge
$13,995 (£8,000)
This features silver-plated copper coil wiring, a platinum magnet, a boron cantilever, plus a body made of coral stone. Listen closely and you can almost hear the waves.

Lyra Atlas phono cartridge
$11,995 (£7,500)
The asymmetrical design apparently improves sound by "suppressing standing waves." Then there's the diamond-coated solid boron cantilever, and the titanium cartridge body. Yikes.

REAL-LIFE NIGHTCLUB

Reality TV star Paris Hilton has had a nightclub constructed in her more-than-opulent Beverly Hills pad. "It used to be a children's playroom before I made it in to the ultimate adult playroom," she says. "I wanted it to look like a club in Paris." Decorated black and gold, it features a high-tech Bose sound system, a bar, a DJ booth, a dancing pole, and a laser, light, and smoke system. Once, for her birthday party, she hired rapper Lil Wayne to perform in the club.

THE GREATEST DANCE SONGS OF ALL TIME

One man's floor filler is another man's sick bucket. Dance music has a habit of attracting more trainspotters than the Orient Express, but if you want to guarantee good times in your man cave nightclub, these 10 classic dance tracks cannot fail to get most people's tail feathers shakin'. They were chosen by the readers of the dance and clubbing magazine *Mixmag*.

10 *Right Here, Right Now* by Fatboy Slim

9 *Xpander* by Sasha

8 *For An Angel* by Paul van Dyk

7 *Spastik* by Plastikman

6 *Music Sounds Better With You* by Stardust

5 *Insomnia* by Faithless

4 *Born Slippy* by Underworld

3 *Smack My Bitch Up* by The Prodigy

2 *Adagio For Strings* by Tiësto

1 *One More Time* by Daft Punk

HOW TO INSTALL A DANCE FLOOR

Your man cave dance floor is going to take a serious battering, especially on 1980s' indie pogo nights. So you'll need a hardwearing sprung wooden surface to absorb it all. Here's an effective DIY version.

1 Remove the top surface of the floor (carpet, vinyl, etc) along with any staples or nails, to reveal the base layer.

2 Buy medium-sized sheets of plywood—enough to cover your entire floor.

3 Glue lots of small foam pads on one side of these sheets of plywood.

4 Lay down the plywood sheets to cover your entire floor (foam pads underneath), staggering them so there are no long joins running across your floor.

5 Lay down a second layer of plywood on top of the first. Secure it in place with long deck screws. Ensure the joins are in a different place to the joins on the first plywood layer.

6 Cover the entire floor with a layer of underlay fabric. The thicker the fabric, the more comfortable and noise-absorbing the carpet will be.

7 Install the hardwood top layer— maple hardwood is a great choice. If you buy it pre-finished, you won't have to varnish it once it's down.

8 Put on your dancing shoes and get down to some serious tunes.

THE SET UP

- Bookcases
- Leather armchairs
- Drinks cabinet
- Cigar humidor
- Antique globe

GENTLEMAN'S CLUB

Here's one gentleman's club where you don't need to apply for membership. Neither do you require a jacket or tie (although that will add to the effect). And if someone doesn't like the cut of your jib, well, you can tell them to get stuffed. This is your own personal gentleman's club, and you can behave exactly the way you want.

Ideally, the walls will be completely lined with bookcases boasting a superb collection of antique tomes. One section of the bookcase could even be a secret door into a second room within your gentleman's club. Leather armchairs are provided for members' comfort. In one corner is a wonderful cabinet of single-malt Scotch whisky and the finest Cognac. In the other is a cigar humidor.

The gentleman's club man cave is reassuringly old-fashioned, as are the gentlemen who frequent it. The general perception of the members of these esteemed venues is of educated sophisticates who get together to discuss the key issues of the day. Behind closed doors, it's more of a case of getting absolutely plastered and drunkenly arguing with your friends. What's not to like?

ROUND THE WORLD

Although the ancient Greeks are known to have produced primitive globes, it wasn't until the planet had been circumnavigated that vaguely accurate renditions were produced. Expensive and difficult to manufacture, they quickly became status symbols of the very rich.

Your man cave is one place that requires such a status symbol. While a quality modern globe will look good (especially if it's dark in there and you have an illuminating model), an antique globe will portray you as a man of the world (literally). Seriously old globes—dating from the 16th century,

for example—show the planet before it was fully explored, with missing islands, incomplete continents, and elements of guesswork here and there.

The best globes are the ones that double up as a drinks cabinet, and no gentleman's club should be without one. Look out for globes at antiques fairs and thrift stores. Failing that, you can get modern versions online.

IT'S HUMID IN HERE

To keep your finest Cubans in tip-top condition, you're going to need a decent humidor. One of the very best (and most expensive) available is manufactured by Swiss brand Imperiali, called the Emperador. Adorn your man cave with this and Colombian drug lords will be jealous.

The Emperador doesn't just keep your cigars at optimum humidity (70 percent) and temperature (60–64°F/16–18°C). No, that would be far too simple. It has been developed with certain ancillary functions designed to further enhance your smoking pleasure.

First up is the cutting mechanism, which uses a laser to determine the perfect length of a cut before guillotining or perforating the cigar, as you prefer. Then there's the lighter; no fumbling around with matches. This device uses three tiny gas rings to create the perfect flame. There's also an in-built ashtray— a vessel that opens automatically when a cigar is brought near.

The price tag? One million Swiss francs ($985,000/£790,000), but then you do get a selection of 24 lovely Honduran and Nicaraguan cigars with your purchase. (Individually wrapped in gold leaf, naturally, inside glass tubes.) And just in case visitors to your man cave can't be trusted, an access code is required to open the humidor.

REAL-LIFE GENTLEMAN'S CLUB

Would Charles Darwin have formulated his brilliant theory of evolution without access to a man cave? Unlikely. He'd surely have been distracted by domestic duties. Fortunately, at his Kent residence, Down House, he enjoyed access to a private study where, among other works, he authored *On the Origin of Species by Means of Natural Selection*. His study has been restored to its original 1870s' set-up and décor, with "almost every original piece of furniture and dozens of his possessions, including some dating from his time on HMS Beagle." The walls are lined with antique books and wooden filing cabinets, while portraits of Darwin's friends hang above a marble fireplace. The desk looks cluttered and well-used, as if the eminent scientist has stepped out of the room for a few minutes. If only all man caves could give rise to such important scientific developments.

HOME
CASINO

THE SET UP

- Poker table
- Roulette table
- Blackjack table
- Craps table
- Slot machine
- Cigar case
- Booze

However strict your local gambling laws happen to be, here's the perfect way to circumvent them: set up your own man cave casino. It's well known that when it comes to gambling the house always wins, so why not make it your house?

When considering the set up for your own mini Caesars Palace, the focal point should be a card table, around which you and your friends will fleece one another for cash late into the night during marathon poker sessions. An ample supply of cigars, beer, whiskey, and snacks must always be nearby. Here's an idea: if you and your friends all chip in a few bucks, you could hire a waiter to keep the refreshments flowing—impoverished teenage sons and daughters are perfect for this job.

Other features of a home casino should include a roulette wheel, a blackjack table, a craps table, and, if you can bear the flashing lights, a slot machine. Not only will this give your casino a more authentic theme, it's a nice little money spinner too. Décor-wise, come up with a theme—ancient Rome, the circus, and pirates are just a few

CASINO HEAVEN

There have been some earth-shattering wins at casinos over the years. (There have also been many catastrophic losses, but let's focus on the positive, shall we?) Here are some of the most legendary victories in the history of gambling.

The Suitcase Man

In 1980, William Lee Bergstrom walked into Binion's Horseshoe Casino in Las Vegas, carrying two suitcases. One contained his life savings in cash of $777,000 (£625,000); the other was empty. He placed the full amount on the craps table on a single bet of dice... And won. According to the casino owner, Ted Binion, who helped him pack his winnings into the two suitcases, Bergstrom had borrowed most of the cash for the bet and planned to commit suicide if he'd lost. Four years later, he won huge amounts again at the same casino. Eventually, as ever, his luck ran out. In November 1984, he lost a million dollars (£800,000) on a single bet. Suicide got him in the end.

found in Vegas—and make sure you've got neon lighting in there somewhere. Also, keep an eye on the time. Many casinos avoid having clocks in the gambling areas, so that patrons lose track of time. Only consider this if you're the kind of guy who doesn't worry about people outstaying their welcome.

The man who broke the bank

Over the summer and fall of 1891, Englishman Charles Deville Wells enjoyed an incredible lucky streak at the Monte Carlo Casino, winning over a million francs (hard to convert into modern currency, but it was a massive win) in the process. His exploits were the inspiration for a popular music hall song of the period called *The Man Who Broke the Bank at Monte Carlo*. Later in his life, Wells was arrested for fraud and eventually died penniless.

50 bucks to $40 million

When it comes to winning streaks, Archie Karas possibly enjoyed the longest ever. An accomplished poker and pool player, he arrived in Las Vegas in 1992 down on his luck and with a betting fund of just $50 (£40). Three years later he had been so unbelievably successful at poker, pool, and craps that he had amassed a total of $40 million (£32 million). Inevitably, the winning streak eventually ended and Karas, gambling with total abandon, lost most of his cash.

17 for 007

As an actor, Sean Connery was very much at home inside casinos – normally sporting a tuxedo, a hidden Walther PPK, and a Martini, shaken, not stirred. But he was also rather fond of betting for real, in his spare time. In 1963, at a roulette table in an Italian casino, he bet on the number 17. When the number came up, he decided to leave his winnings in place. Lo and behold, 17 came up a second time. Recklessly, he left the winnings in place for a third time and incredibly he won again, clearing over 17 million lire. (And that was back when 17 million lire was quite a lot.)

The complete

The number 17 proved to be lucky for billionaire businessman Mike Ashley, too. In 2008, the owner of Sports Direct chain of sporting-goods stores and Newcastle United Football Club won $1.6 million (£1.3 million) in a single spin of the roulette wheel at a London casino. It was thanks to a bet known as a complete. As well as winning on the number 17, he also won by covering black, odd numbers, numbers between one and 18, and every other possible placement that might include 17. His stake totalled $600,000 (£480,000).

The biased wheel

Sometimes the only way to win big is to cheat big. That's what a certain Joseph Jagger did at a famous casino in Monte Carlo back in the 1800s. After paying scouts to observe the casino roulette tables, he realized that one of the wheels was substantially biased, resulting in certain numbers coming up time and time again. So he placed bets on those numbers... Time and time again. Eventually, he walked away with a large fortune. Unfortunately for Jagger, the casino soon noticed the errant wheel and replaced it.

REAL-LIFE HOME CASINO

Rapper 50 Cent used to gamble a lot more than his half-dollar moniker might suggest. At his private mansion in Farmington, Connecticut—one of the largest properties in that entire state—he installed his very own private casino man cave where his friends would attend extravagant gambling parties. The house also featured a helicopter pad, movie theater, basketball court, swimming pools, and no less than 52 rooms. The opulent lifestyle eventually caught up with 50 Cent, however, and he was forced to file for bankruptcy.

FOODIE KITCHEN

The foodie man cave requires a bit of space. Not because food-lovers are fat (although a good proportion of them are certainly well proportioned), but because they will need at least a small kitchenette, a fridge, and a dining area. What's the point of having a foodie man cave if you can't share your delicious creations with other gourmands?

Wannabe chefs have great taste when it comes to food, but they dress scruffily. Not surprising, really, when you consider what ends up all over their clothing. The three key items in a foodie's wardrobe are:

Hat: a baseball cap will do, as long as it keeps hair out of what's cooking, but if there's sufficient headroom in your man cave, why not sport a proper chef's hat?
Apron or chef's whites: avoid anything too kitsch, such as anything with full-frontal nudity.
Clogs: great for protecting toes from accidental knife injury.

What with the sink, cooker, and microwave, your man cave will need to be both plumbed in and wired up for electricity. Keep a fire extinguisher handy for when the crème brûlée gets too brûlée.

Ideally, a foodie man cave should be in the backyard. That way you can build a barbecue, smoker, or pizza oven right outside for some al fresco cooking. A final bit of advice: be wary of cooking fish in a man cave, the smell lingers for days.

THE SET UP

- Sink
- Fridge
- Knives (see right), crockery, and cutlery
- Non-stick frying pan and selection of saucepans in different sizes
- Cooker (gas is best, but restrictions may mean electric is more convenient)
- Microwave
- Trash can
- Barbecue or pizza oven (outside)
- Blow torch
- Fire extinguisher
- Tools: ladle, mixing bowls, wooden spoons, whisk, grater, rolling pin, sieve, scales, etc.
- Cooking essentials: salt, pepper, spices, herbs, oils, etc.

GADGETS

Every self-respecting chef needs a (pointless) gadget or two to keep their foodie man cave ticking over.

Sous-vide machine
For vacuum packing and slow-cooking. Don't be put off by the 10-hours-plus cooking times for a steak—you've seen this on *Masterchef* and it looks delicious.

Ice-cream maker
Used once and then left to gather dust, but you just had to try that sour cherry and ricotta sorbet recipe, didn't you?

Expensive food mixer
You like bread, everyone likes cakes, so why not invest in this device? Because making bread is a massive ball ache and should you be eating that many slices of carrot cake a week?

Dehydrator
You dehydrated everything in your cupboards, then this went into the back of the cupboard, never to be seen again.

CUTTING EDGE

Knife crime in a man cave? That's when you fail to stock the best kitchen knives money can buy.

HOW MANY KNIVES?

Chef's knife
The large handle and blade allows you to chop up lots of vegetables very quickly. Using a rocking motion you can also chop up herbs.

Paring knife
The smaller blade is essential for fiddly jobs, such as peeling fruit.

Bread knife
The serrated edge lets you cut through bread.

Santoku knife
Santoku means "three virtues" in Japanese. It's designed for slicing, dicing, and mincing. Even if you can't wield it properly, you'll look the part.

Carving knife
Great for the Sunday roasts.

CARING FOR YOUR KNIVES

Follow these tips if you really want to cut the mustard.

1   Never put knives in the dishwasher.

2   Wash and dry knives by hand.

3   Don't leave knives soaking in the sink.

4   Never store knives in the cutlery drawer where they can get blunted. A magnetic rack is best. A knife block is good, but it can rub against the blade.

5   Use wooden or plastic chopping boards. Harder materials—such as marble, ceramic, or glass—will damage the blade.

6   Never sharpen with an electric sharpener because it's uneven and removes too much steel. Use a honing steel or a whetstone.

REAL-LIFE FOODIE KITCHEN

In Spain's Basque Country, men have taken the idea of the foodie man cave to a wonderful extreme. They call it the *txoko* (literal translation: "cozy corner"), a gastronomic club where men come together to cook, eat, and no doubt discuss sport. Talk of politics is very much frowned upon. In the traditional *txokos*—often in basement premises with a full kitchen set up—only men are allowed. Some ban women altogether.

The first *txokos* were set up in the 1800s. It was during the Franco regime, from the 1930s until the 1970s, however, that they really flourished since, given the moratorium on political talk, they were one of the few places where the fascist state allowed Basque Spanish to speak their own language and sing Basque songs.

Nowadays, there are many vibrant *txokos* all across the Basque Country, with thousands of gourmand members. The clubs have had a significant impact on Basque cuisine, allowing men to revive traditional recipes and experiment with new variations.

SPORT CAVE

This is surely one of the most popular man caves of all. A sanctuary where males can congregate, drink beer, and watch live sport without interruption.

The best thing about this cave is it's very easy to achieve. At its most basic all you need is a TV screen (ideally three in case of viewing clashes), the larger the better. Surround sound and a fridge stocked with beer and junk food are also key. Since you'll be spending many happy hours watching TV in your man cave, the seats must be extra-comfy, and upholstered with a material that won't get sweaty in summer. The walls should be gloriously decorated with sports memorabilia, plus the obligatory shrine to your favorite team. All visitors will be obliged to pray at said shrine upon entry to your man cave.

THE SET UP

- Multiple TVs
- Fridge
- Reclining seats and sofa
- Sports memorabilia
- Team shrine
- Fire extinguisher
- Cooking essentials

MEMORABILIA TO DIE FOR

According to thesportster.com, the following sports memorabilia are among the most expensive ever sold. Legendary baseball star Babe Ruth features heavily. Imagine if you could decorate your sports man cave with this lot? You'd better start saving now if you fancy putting any of these on the wall.

Babe Ruth's 1920 baseball jersey

$4.415 million (£3.5 million)

It's the oldest known New York Yankees jersey that was actually worn by The Bambino himself. It sold at auction in 2012.

James Naismith's 1891 rules of basketball

$4.3 million (£2.45 million)

Back in 1891, Canadian-born teacher James Naismith invented basketball and codified the rules. His original rulebook is quite an heirloom.

Mark McGwire's 70th home run ball

$3 million (£2.4 million)

Remember this St Louis Cardinals batter's record 70 home runs in 1998? So does everyone else, including the collector who shelled out $3 million for the ball.

Honus Wagner 1909 baseball card

$2.8 million (£2.25 million)

Good old Honus didn't want kids to smoke, so he refused to extend the American Tobacco Company's license to feature him on cigarette cards. This meant very few were ever distributed, guaranteeing the collectibility of the one that, in 2007, sold for $2.8 million.

KICK BACK AND RELAX

Watching sport on the TV in your underpants all afternoon can really take it out of you. What you need is a luxurious reclining armchair. One of the best (and most expensive) is the AcuTouch 9500x massage chair from Californian company Human Touch. Priced at $6,499 (£5,200), it features massage engines for various parts of your body, heaters for your lower back, plus foot and calf wells for your lower legs. Never again will you cramp up while watching the golf. The leather upholstery will withstand a lot of beer spillage, too.

REAL-LIFE SPORT CAVE

Minnesota Vikings tight end Kyle Rudolph lives in a $2.9 million (£2.3 million) mansion near Minneapolis with his girlfriend Jordan and two pet dogs. As you'd expect, his sports-themed man cave in the basement is pretty impressive with a bar, pool table, popcorn machine, and oodles of football memorabilia, including jerseys donated by fellow NFL players. But the *pièce de résistance* is the multiple-reclining-seat movie theater where he spends many an idle hour playing NFL video games.

Paul Henderson's 1972 jersey
$1.275 million (£1 million)
Paul Henderson scored the winning goals in a series of ice hockey matches between Canada and USSR at the height of the Cold War in 1972. This was the jersey he wore.

Babe Ruth's first Yankee Stadium home run bat
$1.265 million (£1 million)
This was the bat that struck the first ever home run in the first ever game played at the original Yankee Stadium. Babe Ruth was the batter who wielded it.

Sheffield FC club rules, regulations, and laws
$1.24 million (£995,000)
Drawn up in 1857, this rulebook belonged to what is now the world's oldest soccer club still competing. It was sold at auction in 2011.

Muhammad Ali vs Floyd Patterson boxing gloves 1965
$1.1 million (£885,000)
He was considered by many as the greatest sportsman of all time. Now that the great man has left us, the price of these gloves will no doubt soon be eclipsed by further Ali memorabilia.

Babe Ruth's 1919 Yankees contract
$996,000 (£800,000)
The New York Yankees paid $100,000 to buy Babe Ruth from the Boston Red Sox in 1919. Who would have thought then that the piece of paper they signed would one day end up as valuable as the player himself?

The FA Cup
$956,000 (£780,000)
Just a handful of Football Association Cup trophies have been made. One version sold for little shy of a million dollars in 2005.

ARTIST'S STUDIO

Daylight is key to any artist's studio, so ideally you want to fit yours with big windows or a skylight. If you have a view from outside your window, even better. A basement will only work if your painting style is going through a black period. Also, below ground level, the humidity may affect your finished pieces.

The equipment and materials you require depend on your medium. If you're working with paint, you'll want an easel and a sink at the very least. What about a potter's wheel or the tool required to create sculptures—welding mask and blowtorch, perhaps?

Creatives like to claim chaos is a sign of genius, but storage should be a key consideration for any artist's studio. Factor in somewhere to keep all the various bits and pieces. Plan chests are perfect for papers and canvases, while charming old apothecary chests have plenty of room for brushes, pencils, and pens. Keep an eye out on eBay for vintage bargains, but really any piece of furniture with lots of drawers and pigeon holes will do.

Planning on painting lots of still life? You might want a dedicated area for your subject matter. Perhaps even a chaise longue for all the nudes you'll have modeling for you.

If you prefer to work digitally, then you'll need a workspace that's big enough to contain a laptop or computer, a good-quality color printer, and possibly a Wacom tablet to aid your illustrations. Graphic designers might also want a storage spot for the thick-rimmed glasses and beard comb.

Finally, ensure you have lots of wall space since this is where you'll be displaying much of your work.

THE SET UP

- Large windows or skylight
- Easel
- Sink
- Potter's wheel
- Canvases
- Painting and drawing materials
- Sculpting materials
- Storage

REAL-LIFE ARTIST'S STUDIO

After he'd saved Europe from the Nazis, Winston Churchill loved nothing better than kicking back with a cigar, a fine wine, and a paintbrush. He was actually a very talented artist and built himself a studio in the garden of Chartwell House, his estate in Kent, where he produced many of his 500 paintings. Aware that his fame might take precedence over his artistic skill, he often displayed art under a pseudonym. Two of his paintings were even accepted by the Royal Academy.

"When I get to heaven I mean to spend a considerable portion of my first million years in painting, and so get to the bottom of the subject," he once said.

REAL-LIFE MAN CAVE

They're not your typical man caves, but they're definitely caves. American artist Ra Paulette has spent much of his lifetime digging caves out of sandstone rocks in the New Mexico desert. With only his dog for company, he has created a series of beautiful subterranean caverns using only hand tools, such as shovels, scrapers, pickaxes, and a wheelbarrow. Many were commissioned by local residents.

"I see this as an environmental project," says Paulette, now in his 60s. "I'm trying to open up people's feelings. But it's pretty down and dirty work."

He describes his caves as a "juxtaposition of opposites." "The sense of being underground with light streaming in," he adds. "The intimacy of being in a cave, yet the columns end up very large, sometimes 30-, 40-feet high."

Paulette's work is now the subject of a documentary film called *Cave Digger*.

MUSIC MAN CAVE

Music fans are by their very nature a noisy lot. At all times they're either listening to loud music, or playing loud music on their instruments. For that reason, it's best if they locate their music man cave at the bottom of the backyard or deep in the basement with loads of soundproofing on the walls. That way they can crank AC/DC up to 11 on the stereo, or strum those Zeppelin riffs on their electric guitars with total impunity.

If music is a crucial enough part of a man's life to justify an entire man cave, then it must be played through a quality sound system. Music fans can get quite obsessive about this, dedicating months of their lives to searching out the very greatest diamond styli, neodymium magnets, and infinite baffle subwoofers, before waxing lyrical about the reassuringly warm sound of vinyl.

You can spot true music fans from a distance. Their torsos are adorned with a T-shirt, normally celebrating some obscure alternative rock band from the 1980s. From their heads will sprout long hair (even if they're balding on the top) tied in a natty little ponytail. From their ears sprout a large and very expensive pair of headphones, or cans, as they call them. They will remove the latter and place them coolly around their necks, but only if required to discuss the finer points of the latest Radiohead album with some other music geek. They tend to wear sunglasses, even indoors on a cloudy day.

THE SET UP

- Sound system (turntable, CD player, MP3 player, amps, speakers)
- Obscenely large collection of records
- Instruments of choice
- Home recording studio
- Listening armchair

HOME RECORDING STUDIO

To record your own music in your man cave, you neither need to break the bank nor get too technical—it's even possible to record something half decent on your phone while on the train to work. Here's an idiot's guide to the basics you will need.

1 An Apple iMac computer or a laptop will do. They're normally the best for home recording.

2 Studio monitor speakers

3 Cables

4 Digital audio workstation software and audio interface. Buy these two together as a combo, because it will work out simpler and cheaper. The former is the software you need, while the latter connects your microphone and instruments to your computer.

5 Microphone

6 Headphones

LP ARTWORK

What with all their streaming and MP3 players, the youth of today will never understand the glorious appeal of album-cover artwork. What are the LP covers that should adorn your man cave walls?

Billion Dollar Babies by Alice Cooper
There's a snakeskin cover, plus a billion-dollar bill inside. Fake of course.

Banana by The Velvet Underground and Nico
"Peel off and see," says the Andy Warhol-created banana on the cover. Saucy!

Look at Yourself by Uriah Heep
There's a real, functioning mirror on the cover.

Metal Box by PIL
Three 12-inch records are packed inside a metal film canister.

Sticky Fingers by The Rolling Stones
Andy Warhol dreamt up this working zipper on a full-to-bursting denim-clad crotch.

Nothing's Shocking by Jane's Addiction
That's provided you're not shocked by the ribbed rubber sleeve.

Ogdens' Nut Gone Flake by Small Faces
The original album was housed in a metal replica of an oversized tobacco tin. It was replaced by a card version after it kept rolling off the shelves.

The Time Of No Time Evermore by The Devil's Blood
This double album was clothbound and emblazoned with gold lettering.

GUITARS

You don't have to be Eric Clapton to appreciate the beauty of a guitar. Even if you can't strum a chord, your cave still needs some axes displayed on its walls. Here are some of the highest-priced models ever known to man.

Custom Rosewood Fender Telecaster
Auction price: $434,750 (£348,750)
Once owned by: George Harrison
The original prototype of this guitar was flown across the Atlantic to George Harrison in 1968 in its own airline seat. The Beatle famously played it on the roof of the Apple Studios in London the following year, in what was to be the band's final live performance.

1958 Gibson Explorer
Estimated value: $500,000 (£400,000)
Once owned by: Eric Clapton
Slowhand, as he was known, bought this guitar—one of only a handful manufactured by Gibson—in 1958, from a fan in Texas.

TURNTABLES

Your exquisite collection of vinyl needs an equally exquisite turntable on which to spin it. Here are three that will cost you pretty much the same as a suburban house. If you choose one of these for your man cave, you'll need security guards and burglar alarms to keep it safe.

AV Designhaus Derenville VPM 2010-1
$650,000 (£460,000)
Possibly the most expensive turntable ever made, this prototype features touch-screen controls, two motors on the belt, four air-suspension feet, and an HD camera to check everything is functioning swimmingly.

Goldmund Reference II
$220,000 (£165,000)
Only 25 of these bad boys were ever made. It includes a liquid-nitrogen-rectified belt. Do you really need that in your man cave? Damn right you do.

Audio Consulting R-evolution Meteor
$172,000 (£138,000)
An entire tree goes into the manufacture of this huge piece of techno-furniture.... One that has been dried for 20 years to avoid any possible warping.

1959 Gibson Flying V
Estimated value: $1 million (£800,000)
Once owned by: Albert King
Gibson manufactured only 17 of these models in 1959, one of which ended up in the dexterous hands of bluesman Albert King. It's now owned by Hollywood actor Steven Seagal.

1959 Les Paul Sunburst
Auction price: $1 million (£800,000)
Once owned by: Keith Richards
This is the axe that "Keef" used to record (I Can't Get No) Satisfaction in 1965. It's rumored to have been stolen from the Rolling Stones guitarist when the band were on tour. In 2006 it was bought by a Swedish collector.

1968 Fender Stratocaster
Estimated value: $2 million (£1.6 million)
Once owned by: Jimi Hendrix
At Woodstock festival in 1969, Hendrix used his fingers (and his teeth) to make this guitar sing. It now graces a museum specially built by Microsoft co-founder Paul Allen who bought it for $1.3 million (£1.05 million). The price has since risen.

SPEAKERS

Crank up your music to full volume in your man cave through some truly gorgeous speakers. To benefit from the full effect, you'll need to set up the system carefully.

Hardwood floors, windows, and glass coffee tables reflect and reverberate the sound, reducing the clarity. On the other hand, extra-thick carpets and lots of upholstered furniture absorb the sound. Aim for something in between. For maximum listening pleasure you can install specially designed acoustic panels.

Ensure the sound your speakers produce is clean by moving the speakers about a foot away from the back wall. For similar reasons, move your listening armchair away from the back wall, toward the middle of your man cave. Angle the speakers so they don't point directly at the opposite wall, but instead turn toward your listening chair. Give your speakers lots of space around them to avoid distorting the sound. Ideally, place them on speaker stands. Here are four of the best speakers money can buy.

Hart Audio D&W Aural Pleasure
$4.7 million (£3.8 million)
Why $4.7 million? It may have something to do with the 24-carat gold cabinets. Don't worry, the sound quality is as pant-wetting as the price.

Transmission Audio Ultimate
$2 million (£1.6 million)
Seven-feet tall and with more woofers than a boarding kennel, this speaker system (according to the manufacturer) "combines the specs of Ferrari, Maserati, and Koenigsegg in one chassis."

Moon Audio Opulence
$1.1 million (£885,000)
Only 10 pairs of these were produced, possibly because of the mind-bending technology that "delivers music into the listener's brain, bypassing the ears." Is that even possible?

Wisdom Audio Infinite Wisdom Grande
$700,000 (£560,000)
You're going to need a reinforced floor on your man cave for this little number. Or large number, rather. It's 13-feet (4-meters) tall and weighs 1.7 tons.

VINYLS YOU MUST OWN
Your man cave may be filled to the rafters with CDs and servers full of digital downloads, but pride of place must be given to your precious collection of vinyl. Here are a few LPs that every vinyl junkie requires.

LPS THAT SOUND BETTER IN ANALOGUE THAN IN DIGITAL
Random Access Memories by Daft Punk
Since a host of famous musicians (Nile Rodgers, Giorgio Moroder, and Pharrell Williams) recorded each of their instruments live, this album always sounds better on vinyl.

Elephant by The White Stripes
Analogue production and a pared down-dirty blues sound mean this is the sort of album that sounds good on CD but just brilliant on vinyl.

The Flying Club Cup by Beirut
Featuring trumpet, flugelhorn, ukulele, accordion, cello, melodica, glockenspiel, upright bass, and tuba, it just doesn't work on any other format.

LPS WITH A NARRATIVE THAT MUST BE HEARD IN THE RIGHT ORDER
• *Dark Side of the Moon* by Pink Floyd
• *Ziggy Stardust* by David Bowie
• *Pet Sounds* by The Beach Boys

DON'T BREAK THE BANK

If you buy only one thing for your music man cave, make it this excellent entry-level DJ-quality turntable—the Pioneer PLX-1000. The high-torque direct drive with an electronic brake makes it easy for mixing, while the dampened platter (with its really cool mirrored dots) lets you dance round your man cave without slipping a disc.

- *Sgt. Pepper's Lonely Hearts Club Band* by The Beatles
- *Kid A* by Radiohead
- *2112* by Rush
- *Back in Black* by AC/DC

LPS WITH SPECIAL FEATURES

Lazaretto by Jack White
Hidden tracks beneath the label, side A playing inside out, a matte finish on side B, a hand-etched hologram... this vinyl may have more special features than any other.

Garden in the City by Melanie
Scratch and sniff cover on this hippie folk offering. "Rub gently to release the magic of Melanie's Garden," it says on the smelly front.

Goodbye Yellow Brick Road by Elton John
Find the yellow plastic double-album version.

King of Limbs by Radiohead
Two slabs of clear vinyl plus a newspaper, CD, and 625 pieces of miniature art. Lovely.

Tea for the Tillerman by Cat Stevens
Get the 200g version which everyone says sounds way better than the normal version.

All Things Must Pass by George Harrison
Generally considered rock's first triple album, revealing a very pent-up ex-Beatle.

Quadrophenia by The Who
Double album and a lavish booklet that takes longer to absorb than the album itself lasts.

REAL-LIFE MUSIC MAN CAVE

Keith Sivyer might well have been the greatest record collector the world has ever seen. Until his death in February 2015, this Londoner religiously purchased every pop single that had featured in the UK record charts from their inception in 1952 until just before he died. That's 45,000 singles in all: 27,000 7-inch vinyl records, 8,000 12-inch records, and 10,000 CD singles.

Every week, he would walk to his local record shop to buy the latest chart entries. When the shop eventually closed he then bought the discs off the Internet. He stored them (alphabetically, of course) in his living room, which, with record players and memorabilia, became his music man cave. Eventually the collection spilled over to fill his entire house, and his floors required reinforcing because of the extra weight.

After Keith's death the collection was sold for $90,000 (£70,000).

Your local multiplex has multi-problems. It's soulless, the popcorn is overpriced, the seats are sticky with spilt drinks, the teenagers are rude, and it rarely shows anything but overblown blockbusters. A home movie theater can trump a multiplex on all these levels.

While a 65-inch high-definition, 3D-compatible flat-screen TV with surround sound will suffice, why not do things properly and go for a full-on projector and 100-inch-plus screen? That way you'll really get the cinema effect. Another area where you mustn't economize is with your seating. Reclining cinema-style seats with drinks holders are obligatory—perhaps a row of five so all your friends can come round for a back-to-back Tarantino marathon.

Other luxuries include a pop-corn machine and some original movie posters on the walls. Of course, the most important thing of all is a vast library of classic movies on DVD and Blu-ray.

HOME MOVIE THEATER

HOME MOVIE THEATER TIPS

While a home cinema of your own is very achievable, it pays to do a bit of planning beforehand—think carefully about the space you have to work with. To get the best movie theater experience, follow these simple tips.

1 A rectangular room with the screen and main speakers on one of the short walls will give you the best set up.

2 Draw black-out blinds or heavy curtains across any windows.

3 Use hanging drapes or furniture to avoid sound reflecting off walls. Concrete walls are the worst. If you're fussy, you can install acoustic panels.

4 Carpet the entire floor to avoid sound echoes.

5 Paint the walls in a dark, matte, neutral color.

6 Low-level ambient lighting will enhance the viewing experience.

THE SET UP

- Projector and screen, or a large TV screen will also work well
- Seating
- Popcorn machine
- Extensive DVD and Blu-ray library
- Movie posters and memorabilia

MOVIE STAR AUTOGRAPHS

Give your home movie theater some star treatment by displaying framed autographs on the walls. The more elusive, and the more dead a film star, the more valuable his or her autograph. So, if your idea of fun is hanging out beside the red carpet at movie premieres in the hope of getting a famous scribble, opt for the coffin dodgers (like Roger Moore, Gene Hackman, Clint Eastwood, Sean Connery, William Shatner— all octogenarians) rather than the youngsters.

According to British memorabilia website Paul Fraser Collectibles, here are some of the most valuable movie star autographs of all time. James Dean tops the list because he died so young and only became globally famous shortly before his death. Therefore he signed very few autographs.

1 James Dean $22,000 (£18,000)
2 Bruce Lee $13,500 (£11,000)
3 Marilyn Monroe $8,700 (£6,950)
4 Charlie Chaplin $6,100 (£4,950)

ROOM WITH A VIEW

Enormous cinema screens won't work if your man cave is quite small. Too wide a screen will have you swinging your head from side to side as if you're at a tennis match. Experts say the best viewing angle is 30 or 40 degrees between eye level and screen level. The ideal viewing distance should place you at a distance from the screen around twice the diagonal width of your screen. This can help you choose what size screen to buy depending on the size of your man cave.

RECYCLING CARDBOARD

You know those giant cardboard cutouts you see in movie theaters promoting the forthcoming features? These can make the perfect addition to your movie man cave. To secure one, speak to an employee at your local theater and express your interest, they will then take your details and once the movie has finished showing you can come and collect it. They may ask for a small payment, so be prepared to negotiate, but often there's no charge as they'll only end up being thrown in the trash.

Be quick though, particularly for big summer blockbusters. You can bet there'll be a few film geeks who also have their eyes on the prize.

CULT MOVIE COLLECTION

Forget the blockbusters and the classics. If you want friends to be really impressed by your home movie theater man cave and want to take your movie geekiness to new levels, you need the ultimate collection of cult movies on DVD. (Or, follow Quentin Tarantino's lead and get them on VHS.) According to *Rolling Stone* magazine, here are the top 10 cult films of all time.

REAL-LIFE HOME THEATER

Fancy a home movie theater that boldly goes where no cinema has gone before? Marc Bell, producer of musicals and former owner of *Penthouse Magazine*, has given his private movie theater a *Star-Trek* theme. As you sit in the beige armchairs, with a control panel in front of you, it feels like you're at the helm of the USS Enterprise. Actually, you're in a very large mansion in Florida.

10 *DONNIE DARKO*
Remember the huge, scary bunny?

9 *PHANTOM OF THE PARADISE*
This Brian De Palma flick is a rock version of Phantom of the Opera.

8 *THE EVIL DEAD*
Sam Raimi dropped out of college to make this demon classic.

7 *PINK FLOYD—THE WALL*
Bob Geldof stars in this surreal, psychedelic rock movie. Best viewed on mind-altering substances.

6 *HAROLD AND MAUDE*
Black comedy about a romance between a young man and an old woman.

5 *A CLOCKWORK ORANGE*
Stanley Kubrick's violent tale of droogs and dystopian crime.

4 *PULP FICTION*
Tarantino's crime movie was so popular that many might see it as mainstream rather than cult.

3 *THIS IS SPINAL TAP*
This mockumentary of course scores 11 out of 10.

2 *THE BIG LEBOWSKI*
Duuuude!

1 *THE ROCKY HORROR PICTURE SHOW*
Fancy dress is obligatory when you watch it.

3D OR NOT 3D (TV)?

Now that really is the question. Given that 3D is such a divisive medium, it ultimately comes down to personal choice. Consider what sort of movies you most like to watch—if it's the latest blockbuster then 3D might be the way to go, but if you're more of an indie lover it's probably not worth it. One thing's for sure, the picture quality on most 3D or regular screens should be top notch.

GEEK DEN

Don't be afraid to embrace your inner geek. All men are a little bit nerdy at heart, so there's no shame in celebrating that geekiness with a full-on man cave.

This Temple to the Nerd should include a kick-ass movie collection (you never know when you'll need to watch *Blade Runner* director's cut for the 37th time), board games that require at least a week to complete (*Dungeons and Dragons*, for example), some classic comic books (including a sub-section on Franco-Belgian *bandes dessinées* from the 1950s), and the most collectible sci-fi figurines known to man (that $2^1/_2$-inch 1977 Darth Vader really is exquisite). Oh, and don't forget the 1:50 scale model of the Millennium Falcon.

Putting together your den is easy. Get a table for gaming, a TV for viewing, a cabinet for displaying, and a comfy chair for reading, then you're good to go.

THE SET UP

- DVDs and Blu-rays
- Board games
- Comic books
- Sci-fi figurines
- Fast Internet connection

THE MOST COLLECTIBLE COMICS

Unsurprisingly, American superhero comics dominate this list. According to *Comic News*, these are the five most expensive comic titles ever sold. Most were close to mint condition.

5 *The X-Men*, **issue 1**
$493,000 (£400,000)
Created by Stan Lee and Jack Kirby, this is the first in the X-Men series.

4 *Batman*, **issue 1**
$567,000 (450,000)
"All brand new adventures of the Batman and Robin, the boy wonder!" And an all brand new price for this 1940 comic that broke the half a million dollars barrier.

3 *Detective Comics*, **issue 27**
$1.07 million (£865,000)
Sold for 10 cents in 1939, this offers a staggeringly good return on your original investment. It was the first appearance of Batman.

2 *Amazing Fantasy*, **issue 15**
$1.1 million (£885,000)
This shocked the comic-book world when it fetched over a million dollars at auction in 2011.

1 *Action Comics*, **issue 1**
$3.2 million (£2.6 million)
Superman made his debut in this 1938 comic, which sold on eBay in 2014 for well over three million dollars.

BEST SCI-FI FILMS OF ALL TIME

Certain profound questions about the cosmos will never be truly answered. Do androids dream of electric sheep? Is Boba Fett really the coolest character in *Star Wars*? Was the sexual tension between Captain Kirk and Lieutenant Uhura based on any real-life romance?

Similarly, nerds will never agree on which sci-fi films are the greatest of all time. In any case, who should be the ultimate judge? Can anyone really say with confidence which sci-fi films we'll all still be watching once we've colonized the rest of the solar system? Well, *Esquire* magazine has had a good attempt at answering this conundrum. According to them, the top 5 best sci-fi films of all time are:

5 *Metropolis* **(1927)**
This German expressionist silent movie was made during the Weimar Republic, with art direction drawing from Cubism, Futurism, and Bauhaus. One of the earliest feature-length sci-fi films, it set in our minds many enduring ideas as to what the future might look like.

4 *Aliens* **(1986)**
The 1979 original, *Alien*, is favored by critics, but the all-out action, explosions, and violence of this follow-up make it the fans' choice.

3 *Gattaca* **(1997)**
This thought-provoking film about eugenics and genetic engineering initially flopped at the box office, but has achieved cult status in the intervening years.

2 *Blade Runner* **(1982)**
Ridley Scott's tale of a dystopian LA in which blade runners hunt down errant replicants has more director's cuts than it has plot twists, only adding to its legendary status among loyal fans.

1 *2001: A Space Odyssey* **(1968)**
If this Stanley Kubrick tale of human evolution doesn't blow your mind, then you probably don't have a mind to blow.

FIGURINES? GO FIGURE

When it comes to collectible figurines, as ever it's rarity that makes them valuable. The discontinued Captain James T. Kirk model with the Starfleet emblem printed upside down, for example. Or the *Doctor Who* baddie who was immortalized in resin but never actually made it into the TV series.

Of all the sci-fi film figurines, *Star Wars* normally commands the highest prices. According to the wealth-obsessed website www.richest.com, these are the most valuable you can find. Ransack your attic to find them. Surely you owned some of these a long time ago in a galaxy far away.

Blue Snaggletooth
Approximate value $600 (£480)
Part of a little-known set of figurines that celebrated the cantina band scene in the original *Star Wars*, the Snaggletooth was mostly manufactured in small red versions. The rarer large, blue ones are significantly more valuable.

Luke Skywalker, with telescopic lightsaber
$1,000 (£800)
A rare early version of Luke Skywalker featured a telescopic-action lightsaber in his right hand. On later more common models he wielded a solid saber.

Han Solo, with blaster gun
$1,000 (£800)
The original version was armed with a blaster—and is now armed with an impressive intergalactic price tag.

Yak Face
$1,000 (£800)
You may have forgotten this little chap—he played a minor role alongside Jabba the Hutt in *Return of the Jedi*—but don't forget his value, which was inflated after he was discontinued.

Boba Fett
$2,000 (£1,600)
Released via a special offer one year before he actually appeared on screen (in 1980's *The Empire Strikes Back*), this super-cool bounty hunter was really popular with fans.

Vlix
$4,000 (£3,200)
Manufactured in a small series by Brazilian modelers Glasslite, this unusual character from the animated series *Star Wars: Droids* is exceptionally rare and gets geeks exceptionally hot in the underpants region.

Obi-Wan Kenobi and Darth Vader with telescopic lightsabers
$7,000 (£5,500)
Everyone loved Obi-Wan. Everyone feared Darth Vader. And they loved and feared them even more when they came with (the easily damaged) telescopic lightsabers.

Medical Droid FX-7
$12,000 (£9,600)
Hailing from the British manufacturer Palitoy, this forgettable droid made a fleeting appearance in *The Empire Strikes Back* when he attended to an injured Skywalker. For some bizarre reason one model sold for nearly $12,000 in 2014. Perhaps, like Luke, the buyer needed a new arm.

Jawa with vinyl cape
$18,000+ (£14,500)
The early vinyl-caped Jawas were quickly given new cloth capes after the initial manufacturing run. The very rare originals are now among the most valuable sci-fi figurines in the galaxy. In any galaxy, in fact. Geeks will use the dark side of the Force to get their hands on this little gem. Beware pirated versions on eBay.

GAMER CAVE

With video gaming now elevated to professional status around the world, the ante has been well and truly upped when it comes to the gaming cave. No windows are required, so your cave is well suited to a basement or attic, where you can happily hunker down for a 12-hour marathon of *Call of Duty*.

The main screen must, of course, be both large and high-quality so as to display your players in all their glory. The number of seats you have depends on how many gamers you plan to invite round, but ensure they are comfortable enough to relax in for all-night sessions, with reclining functions.

To give your cave character, what about some vintage arcade games? Activate the coin slots, invite your friends round, and rake back some of that small fortune you spent on *Street Fighter II* and *Virtua Cop* as a kid.

THE SET UP

- Console and large screen
- Reclining seats and/or gaming chairs
- Vintage arcade games

INTERIORS

You need to decorate your cave according to your favored style of game—this will give you a psychological edge while playing. So if *Grand Theft Auto* is your cup of tea, go for the deprived inner-city look. If it's *Call of Duty* that really floats your boat, how about a full-on military makeover complete with genuine US military combat uniforms? Fans of *Elder Scrolls* or *World of Warcraft* might opt for some medieval interior design.

GAMING CHAIRS

Face facts, you're going to spend a LOT of time sat in the same spot, so you might want to think about investing in a dedicated chair to park your backside. Ergonomically designed and insanely comfortable, these gaming chairs mean you can theoretically spend endless hours playing *FIFA* or *Madden*.

Gaming chairs really come into their own for fans of racing games, with simulations of the seats and driving positions you find in rally and F1 cars. Add in some responsive, real-feel pedals and a steering wheel and it's just like driving the real thing.

REAL-LIFE GAMER CAVE

Southeast Asia has some of the most obsessive video games man caves on the planet, known as gaming houses. Whole teams of professional e-sportsmen live together in these houses, where they eat, drink, and breathe video games for almost every waking hour of the day.

One of the most impressive is the huge Filipino gaming house called Mineski. It is home to professional teams specializing in *League of Legends*, *Dota 2*, and *Counter-Strike: Global Offensive*, who stay there for months on end, honing their skills. Pale of skin, sore of thumb, and red of eye, the e-sportsmen (and they are mostly men... Of the teenage variety) have access to different learning rooms and lightning-fast Internet connections. The team organizers describe the house as "a decisive move to help them get closer to their goal of becoming the best team in the world."

GET A HEAD IN THE GAME

Any self-respecting gamer needs a serious headset. Not only can you get quality 7.1 surround sound just through a pair of headphones, it also gives you the chance to get into verbal battles with eight-year-old Korean kids kicking your butt at *League of Legends*.

However, hardcore gamers will be looking at a different type of headset—the VR (virtual reality) headset. This offers a truly immersive 360-degree gaming experience, and although at the time of writing VR gaming is in its infancy, there's a good chance this represents the future. Therefore, it's a must-have for your man cave. If VR goes the way of the Dreamcast or NeoGeo, there'll be some cult kudos earned by owning a gaming flop.

THE BEST VINTAGE ARCADE GAMES

Did you spend countless hours of your youth, and the majority of your pocket money, battling crudely pixelated aliens, ghosts, and street ruffians? Of course you did. That's why you now need to relive your youth by installing classic arcade games in your man cave. The following games (from what's often referred to as the golden age of arcade video games) may no longer ramp up the adrenalin levels they once did, but as a snapshot of 20th-century youth culture, they are glorious.

If the original arcade machines are beyond your budget, try searching on eBay for console versions. Handily, Nintendo have recently released the Nintendo Classic Mini, a replica of the original NES console. It comes loaded with three of the games recommended here, plus 27 additional classics.

Space Invaders

This was the game that ushered in the golden age of arcade games. And in what style! Remember the joystick-gripping tension as row after row of soulless aliens attempted to invade your planet? And the ominous marching sound as they slowly but inexorably accelerated their approach? It was the stuff of nightmares... For an eight-year-old, at least.

Pac-Man

Is this the most famous arcade game of all time? So simple—you eat the pac-dots and avoid the ghosts—yet so effective and addictive.

Street Fighter

It's the late 1980s. You're a teenaged, bespectacled weakling, dotted with acne, but give yourself half an hour on *Street Fighter* and you feel like you could take on Chuck Norris.

Donkey Kong

The hero (Mario) had to rescue the damsel in distress (Pauline) from a giant ape (Donkey Kong). Some of the most bonkers ideas are the best. Genius.

Mario Bros

Who'd have thought that two Italian-American plumbers from New York could get kids so excited?

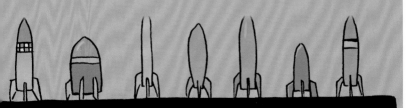

TRAIN SET AND MODELING CAVE

The life of a model railway maker sometimes can be hard, having to be the butt of your friends' and family's gags about your passion. However, once they've got past all the trainspotting jokes and actually tried one out, they'll realize that train sets are pretty cool. As a centerpiece of any man cave, they work gloriously—a combination of machinery and modeling that can be added to and upgraded as the years go by. The other bonus of the train set is that it doesn't require much vertical space, so it works perfectly in the limited-ceiling-height room of a loft or a basement.

Model railway enthusiasts (sorry, there's just no cool way of describing train-set fans) traditionally have a rather nerdy image: anoraks, dorky shoes, thick-rimmed glasses, and an unhealthy obsession with train timetables. But if you're going to spend thousands on a state-of-the-art model train set, isn't it about time that nerdy image got an upgrade? What about a classic train-driver's uniform? Maybe something from Revolution-era Russia, with leather waistcoat and peaked cap, or the hickory-striped dungarees and hat of a stoker on the Union Pacific? A whistle and flag will add to the overall effect.

While your model railway can be in the loft, the best model-making man caves will also need a work surface where you can create your models. These don't just have to be trains, you can use the surface for modeling boats, aeroplanes, tanks, and perfect renditions of the Empire State Building made out of Lego. The key considerations are to have a steady surface to support your steady hand, a good source of light (whether natural or a desk lamp), and space to keep tools, such as cutting knives, pliers, paint, and glue.

Don't forget to have plenty of secure places to hide your tiny modeling pieces, particularly if there's a risk that kids (and their tiny meddling hands) might find their way into your cave.

THE SET UP

- Train set and other models to work on
- Work surface
- Paint, glue, and tools

THE WORLD'S MOST AMAZING TRAIN SET

Professional modelers have spent over half a million man hours and nearly $15 million (£12 million) creating by far the largest and most jaw-dropping train set on the planet. Housed in the warehouse district of the German city of Hamburg, it's called Miniatur Wunderland, and it's still growing.

At the time of writing, there were eight different areas to the visitor attraction, spread out across over 4,000-square feet (1,300-square meters). They included scale reproductions of train networks in alpine mountains, Hamburg itself, USA, Scandinavia, Switzerland, and a commercial airport. More areas—"Italy, France, and probably England"—are planned by the year 2020. Eventually there will be over 12 miles of track, around 1,300 trains, 20,000 wagons, 6,000 buildings and bridges, 330,000 trees, and 400,000 figurines.

Miniatur Wunderland is the brainchild of twin brothers, Frederik and Gerrit Braun. Model railway fans as kids, they started building their miniature world back in 2000, opening a year later.

"Most of our friends considered us as crazy quixotic dreamers when we told them about our idea," says Frederik. Gerrit adds: "Model railways were considered an antiquated hobby of loners, but our idea was to create a world which likewise inspires men, women, and kids to dream and marvel."

And it seems to have worked. Well over 10 million visitors have marveled at their work so far.

THE WORLD'S BIGGEST MATCHSTICK MODEL

Have you perhaps got 15 years to spare, and over four million matchsticks? That's what was required of British modeler David Reynolds, who currently holds the Guinness World Record for the world's largest matchstick model.

His creation, which weighs in at a ton and is 12-feet high and 20-feet long (3.6 by 6.1 meters), depicts a North Sea oil platform, and is now on display in Reynolds' home town of Southampton. It's a subject the 51-year-old knows a fair bit about, having spent much of his career working on oil rigs himself.

"People sit in front of the television for five or six hours a night, but I get bored so I'd just nip off for a few hours here and there to work on it," he said of the model, which he constructed in various rooms around his house. "It just started as a bit of a hobby, but I guess it got out of hand. It's good fun and keeps the gray matter working."

His wife Julie isn't quite so keen. "I am absolutely sick to death at the sight of a matchstick," she said. "But I think there is still more to come, unfortunately."

She's not wrong. Reynolds has since embarked on a new model— an armada of matchstick ships.

PHOTOGRAPHY STUDIO

So you've mastered the selfie and your Instagram pictures are getting at least 10 likes a time. Sounds like it's time for you to start setting up your own photography studio.

Since you're always supplying your own light, a studio can be in the attic, basement, spare room, garden shed... Anywhere. The bulk of the man cave will be taken up by a backdrop (one you can roll away after use) or, even better, an infinity curve. Make sure you have enough space in the studio to be able to zoom when you need to; a minimum depth of 15 feet (4.3 meters) should work. Then there's all the photographic equipment, including cameras, tripod, lights, light-stands, light modifiers, reflectors, umbrellas, etc. On the walls of your studio you want to show off your best work.

Digital technology means you can now get away with smaller studios, since a darkroom is no longer required. But some old-school snappers still love print film, in which case they'll need a separate darkroom area for processing.

THE SET UP

- Backdrop
- Cameras
- Lights, light-stands, light modifiers, reflectors, umbrellas, tripod

PICKING A CAMERA

Whether you're shooting stills or video, there's a baffling amount of choice out there and the price of camera hardware can quickly become very scary indeed. Fear not. Here are two quality entry-level cameras—one still and one a still-video hybrid—that won't break the bank.

Nikon D3300
Around $450 (£340)

This camera boasts the same professional-level features as some top-of-the-range Nikon cameras, but it's compact and light enough to work well with amateurs too. It comes with a 24.2 mega pixel image sensor and a built-in flash.

JVC GC-PX100
Around $1,000 (£700)

This camcorder-camera hybrid can shoot video in full high definition and capture high-speed footage. The time-lapse video mode makes for great film effects. An app allows you to review footage on your phone.

If money's no object, take a look at this model:

Canon 5DS R
Around $3,900 (£3,000)

This beast is perfect for the studio, packing a huge 50.6 megapixels, giving you insanely high-resolution images. It's also no slouch when it comes to landscape photography. Be warned, the price is just for the body, you'll have to buy lenses on top of that!

BUILDING YOUR STUDIO

The camera never lies, or so they say, but the same can't be said for the studio. If you've never stepped into a professional photography studio, you'd be forgiven for expecting pristine walls, beautiful wooden floors, immaculate sets... While some are indeed like this, many studios are an absolute tip, so don't worry about the state of the space you've set aside to shoot. Instead, focus on these simple tips that'll ensure you'll be able to snap like the pros.

Room to zoom
Your man cave must be deep enough so that you can use a variety of lenses, and so you can step back and zoom in if you need to. For full-body shots, the minimum depth you'll need is about 15 feet (4.5 meters).

Tripod
Some shots are perfect for freehand photography, but for those where you are shooting in macro, close up to your subject, or need a long exposure time, a good-quality tripod is essential.

Ceilings not too low
Otherwise they act as a giant reflector. Paint them a dark color to reduce stray light.

Cover the windows
Sometimes you'll love the natural daylight that streams in through a window in your man cave—it can add to the effect. Other times you'll want to block it out entirely with blackout blinds or thick curtains.

Studio lights
You'll need a main light with a soft box (or umbrella) to make the shadows less harsh when you need to. If you're shooting models, you might want to position a hair light at the back.

Reflectors
These are used to redirect light to or from a subject. They can be as basic as a piece of polystyrene or you can invest in something a bit more professional.

Clamps and stands
For holding the above and backdrops.

Backdrop
Ideally, you should make room at one end of your studio for a wall mount, or stands from which you can hang paper backdrops. Keep a selection of different-colored and textured backdrops to shoot with.

Props
Keep lots of props in your studio. Random furniture, crockery, clothing, jewelry, and accessories will give you options for different shoots.

Laptop
Even at amateur level, it's good to use a tethering cable or Wi-Fi link to transfer photos from your camera to your laptop. That way you can monitor the exposure, the framing, the props, and the models' expressions as you shoot. They are also essential for post-production software, like Adobe Photoshop, where you can tweak your images to your heart's content.

PUB GAMES ROOM

Playing a few games of pool while enjoying a pint or two is one of life's great pleasures, but spending hours at the local can get you in a spot of bother with your better half. If this scenario sounds familiar, why not create your own version of the pub at home? That way you'll get the best of both worlds.

For many, the pub games room is the ultimate man cave. There's something wonderful about sports you can play while you drink. Pool, darts, skittles, fruit machines, quiz machines, arcade games... Yes, these are indeed sports. And, yes, you do improve at all of them the more beer you consume. There is a downside to this cave in that you do need quite a lot of room in order to fit in the pool table, but if space is not an issue then what's stopping you?

Place your pool table in the center of your man cave, so you have plenty of elbow room. There's nothing more infuriating than having to make way for a fellow drinker just as you're lining up to sink the black. For darts you need at least 7 feet $9^1/_4$ inches (2.37 meters) between the board and the oche. This area could also double up for a small version of pub skittles. Elsewhere, you can install your retro *Space Invaders/Pac-Man* arcade table and perhaps a fruit machine.

Finally, don't forget the actual bar. This can be anything from a well-stocked fridge and a space to perch with a pint to a fully functioning bar complete with kegs and hand pumps. As long as there's beer readily available, you and your patrons will be more than happy. A few bar snacks also wouldn't go amiss—jars of pickled eggs are surprisingly good value these days.

THE SET UP

- Pool table
- Darts board
- Retro arcade games
- Fruit machine
- Quiz machine
- Bar
- Fridge

REAL-LIFE PUB GAMES ROOM

Yorkshireman Chris Embling built his games room man cave in tribute to his son, Rory, who died suddenly at the age of 26. It's designed in the style of a country pub, named Rory's Return, with a jukebox and plenty of signed football shirts and memorabilia adorning the walls. In fact, it's all so impressive that it won the 2015 Home Leisure Direct Games Room of the Year competition.

COOL WITH POOL

Pool has to be the most popular pub sport and acquiring a table of your own should be a top priority. Sometimes it's best to furnish your man cave with a cheap second-hand pool table, especially if beer and ash are going to be spilled on a regular basis. Just imagine, though, what your games room might look like with one of these gracing it.

X1 Everest
Price on application
The transparent playing surface replicates the feeling of playing on felt and "gives the impression the table is floating on air." Made by Australian brand Elite Innovations.

BlackLight
$34,800 (£28,000)
This French design from Billards Toulet features internal lighting and a jukebox. When you're bored of pool you can quickly convert it into a dining table or a poker table.

The Luxury Billiard
$177,000 (£143,000)
Designed by pool champion Vincent Facquet together with Billards Toulet, this has backlit pockets, gold or platinum leafing, and diamonds positioned along the railing.

Obscura Cuelight
$200,000 (£161,000)
The table's lighting system allows you to project images onto the cloth. It can even track the movement of the balls and animate them with lighting effects as they move.

REAL-LIFE PUB GAMES ROOM

When he lived in Hartford, Connecticut, in the late 1800s, author Mark Twain transformed the entire top floor of his house into one massive billiards room. This is where he would retreat with his male friends to pot balls, smoke cigars, and imbibe brown spirits. His wife and children were, of course, barred entry.

"There ought to be a room in this house to swear in," said the creator of Tom Sawyer and Huckleberry Finn. "It's dangerous to have to repress an emotion like that. Under certain circumstances, profanity provides a relief denied even to prayer."

God knows he's f* * *ing right about that one.

STAY SHARP

You might think that one dart is much the same as another, but no self-respecting player would line up at the oche without his own set of arrows, complete with flights of his favorite sports team, brewery, or brand of bar snack.

If you really want to go to town (and since this is your man cave, we highly encourage you to do so), then consider investing in customized darts. The budget option is to create a mix-and-match set made up of different tips and shafts, but for the truly bespoke experience favored by the pros, companies will analyze your playing style and create a set of darts that are completely unique to you. At around $1,500 (£1,250) for three arrows it's not cheap, but can you put a price on the joy of your first nine-dart finish?

HOME BREWERY

THE SET UP

- Home-brewing equipment—a ready-made kit or all-grain set up
- Fermentation vessels
- Sink
- Heat source/cooking hob
- Extractor fan
- Cleaning and sterilizing materials
- Bottles
- Storage for bottles
- Bar area
- Fridge
- Beer mats
- Urinal

The price of beer, eh? It's scandalous. One solution is to create your own micro-brewery in your man cave. Men have been brewing beer in their caves since Neolithic times. Although, back then, the quality wasn't perhaps what it is now. With your very own micro-brewery you will be able to invest lots of time and practice into your passion. Who knows? Get your zymurgy right (that's the science of brewing, by the way, and a very impressive Scrabble score) and one day you may create a home brew so good you can actually sell it.

Brewing is actually surprisingly easy—all you need is a home-brewing kit. There are hundreds available online, catering for every beer taste, some involving just the addition of water and a few ingredients. If you want to get serious about beer, then full-mash, all-grain brewing is the way to go. For this you'll need to invest in some equipment—a boiler, mash tun, and fermentation vessel make up your basic set up, plus bottles to put your brew in. You're also going to need a cooking hob/heat source and ideally an extractor fan so you can air out your man cave. You'll then need to set aside some space for storing your hops and malt and, of course, your finished bottles, plus a small area for drinking them. If possible, install a urinal in one corner of your beer man cave. You know what they say: once you break the seal.

SMALL-SPACE BREWING

If you want to brew but are lacking space, don't panic because help is at hand with the Braumeister. Manufactured by German company Spiedel, this all-in-one brewing system allows you to mash and boil in the same vessel. It also avoids the need for sparging as it circulates the wort automatically, meaning you can just sit back and wait for your beer to brew. It comes in 10-liter, 20-liter, and 50-liter versions, so pick the size that works best for your cave. Of course, such a serious piece of kit comes with a suitably serious price tag, but it will certainly impress visitors to your cave, as will the quality of your produce.

WHAT TO BREW?

In need of some recipe inspiration? Then look no further than Scottish brewery BrewDog, who have released the recipes for every beer they've ever brewed; for free. That's over 200 hundred different beers, covering a multitude of different styles—from lagers and IPAs to imperial stouts and porters. Should keep you busy for a while.

BEER-TASTING TIPS

Just like fine wines, great beers need to be treated with respect. Here are tips to enhance beer-tasting sessions in your man cave.

Before you drink

- Start off by drinking mild, light beers, such as pale ales. Finish with the rich, bitter ones, like imperial stouts and porters. This will allow your taste buds to get accustomed to the increasingly stronger flavors.

- As a general rule, beers that are lighter in body and lower in alcohol should be drunk cold, while those that are fuller in body and heavier in alcohol should be drunk at a warmer temperature. According to *Craft Beer & Brewing Magazine*, here are the ideal serving temperatures for different beers:

- Commercial light lagers: 35–40°F (2–4°C)
- Pilsners and wheat beers: 40–45°F (4–7°C)
- Pale ales, porters, and stouts: 45–50°F (7–10°C)
- Belgian ales, bocks, bitters, and milds: 50–55°F (10–13°C)
- Barley wines, imperial stouts, and strong ales: 55–60°F (13– 16°C)

- Human taste buds are normally at their most alert state around midday, which is a damn fine excuse for a boozy lunch in your man cave.

- Use the correct glasses. Light, blonde beers are best out of tall, thin glasses with a small surface area so as to retain the fizziness. Rich, strong ales are best drunk from goblets, so that your nose can appreciate the full flavor as you drink.

- Avoid smoking or wearing aftershave, since it masks the real flavor of the beer.

- Cleanse your palate in between beers with bread, unsalted crackers, or cold water.

- Allow a decent head to form on top of the beer—a depth of two fingers will suffice. This will let you appreciate the aroma.

As you drink

- Before taking your first sip, examine the color, head, and consistency of the beer. Avoid holding it up directly in front of a light source as this will change its true color.

- Swirl the beer gently in its glass. This will release aromas, encourage the bubbles, and ensure a decent head. Notice whether the head is dense or thin. If it has dips and peaks in it, you can describe it as "rocky."

- Breathe in the beer's aroma deeply through your mouth and nose.

- Take a large sip of the beer and allow it to move around your mouth. Feel its consistency, its flavor, its bitterness. Try to describe the initial taste. Does it have a citrus taste? Is it chocolatey, or malty? Peppery? Burnt coffee?

- Notice the lingering flavor after you have swallowed the beer.

KEEP IT CLEAN

It's common for men not to pay much attention to their appearance— a bit of dirt, dishevelment, and man scent never did anyone any harm. This is not the case when it comes to making beer; here cleanliness really is next to godliness. Speak to any home brewer and they'll tell you how crucial it is to sterilize all your gear before you brew. They will all share a certain look in their eye as they tell you this information. It harks back to the trauma of saying goodbye to a brew that's been rendered undrinkable by an infection. Don't let the same thing happen to you.

BARISTA'S COFFEE HOUSE

Disappointed by the dull array of franchise coffee shops on your high street? It's time to get serious and create your very own coffee man cave—a domestic temple to the mighty bean.

There are certain practicalities to think of. A coffee man cave cannot exist without a seriously sexy espresso machine, preferably Italian, so make sure you have both water and electricity. You'll also need a small sink to wash up all the coffee cups.

The opportunities for coffee paraphernalia are awesome. Flea markets should be mined for items such as antique stove-top coffee pots, pre-War Italian café signs, and unusual espresso cups. All perfect for decorating your coffee man cave.

THE SET UP

- Espresso machine
- Aeropress or pour-over filter coffee maker
- Cafetière/French press
- Expensive coffee
- Grinder
- Cups
- Sink
- Barista's apron

WORLD'S MOST EXPENSIVE COFFEE

When selling a single cup of coffee for between $35 and $100 (£30 and £80) a cup, you don't expect customers to tell you "it tastes like sh*t." However, with kopi luwak coffee, they would in fact be correct. For this particular brew is made from coffee beans first eaten and then defecated by mammals indigenous to Southeast Asia called Asian palm civets.

It turns out said civets love nothing more than munching on tasty coffee berries. During the ensuing digestive process, the flesh of the berries is removed, but the beans inside remain undigested. Even better, the enzymes inside the civet cat's intestines somehow render the beans less acidic and bitter. Post-poop, it makes for a much smoother and more flavorsome taste.

All of which begs the question, how on earth did Southeast Asians first discover that the beans in civet cat feces would produce such a lovely brew? Back in the 19th century, when Indonesia was a Dutch colony, all the normal coffee beans were exported back to Europe and the locals weren't allowed a sniff. They weren't banned from rummaging around in civet cat poop, however, and that's when they discovered the unique taste of excreted beans.

In northern Thailand there's a similarly produced coffee brand called Black Ivory Coffee. In this case, it's elephant rather than civet poop that is responsible for the lovely taste.

STEAMING MILK

To make great milk-based coffees you need to be able to steam milk correctly. Here's how:

- Fill a metal jug to just over halfway with full-fat milk. Give the steam wand of your espresso maker a quick blast to clear any condensation and then place it in the jug; the tip should just break the surface.

- Turn on the steam again, angling the flow to create a whirlpool in the milk. The tip should remain just below the surface of the milk and no large bubbles should form.

- Once the milk begins to thicken, lower the wand further into the milk and continue to heat until the side of the jug is hot to touch. Tap the jug on a work top to break surface air bubbles, give the foam a quick swirl to combine, and it's ready to pour into/combine with your espresso.

HOW TO PIMP YOUR COFFEE

You don't need the help of a professional barista to make a damn fine cup of joe in your man cave. Follow these tips to seriously improve the quality of your brews.

1 Buy great beans
Don't scrimp on quality. Many websites now offer high-grade roasts from countries all round the world.

2 Buy small amounts
Coffee beans quickly date, so purchase little and often rather than in bulk.

WHAT KIND OF COFFEE MACHINE DO YOU NEED?

Yes, you can splash out thousands on a commercial Gaggia coffee machine but unless you're planning to open a café, it's a touch extravagant, even for the very best man cave. A domestic machine will suffice. There are three basic types you can opt for:

1 A manual espresso machine, where you fill the filter with ground coffee. These are compact versions of the commercial machines you find in cafés.
2 A bean-to-cup machine which grinds the coffee and pours it automatically.
3 A capsule machine, where you place a ready-made capsule in the machine and let it do all the work.

If you want to impress guests in your man cave, go for option 1. Option 3 is far too convenient for a serious barista.

BREWING ALTERNATIVES

Ask a barista what they drink at home and the answer is often "not espresso." Here are some other options for your morning cup:

Aeropress
This easy-to-use coffee "syringe" uses air pressure to brew seriously good coffee. It's also self-cleaning—how can you argue with that?

Pour-over filter coffee
Simple yet devastatingly effective, filter brewing produces sweet, tasty coffee for next to nothing.

Stove-top aka Moka pot
Stove-top coffee has an unfair rep, being thought of as bitter, over-extracted sludge. In reality, the Moka can make a deliciously strong coffee.

Cafetière aka French press
There's a reason why this is so popular—the immersive brewing method gives a full-bodied cup.

3 Grind
Buy a grinder and grind the beans yourself to guarantee freshness. If you want to geek out, buy a conical-burr grinder. These ensure a truly consistent grind and, unlike blade grinders, don't raise the temperature of the beans during the grinding process. This reduces unwanted bitter flavors in your cup. Conical-burr hand grinders are cheap to buy and have the added bonus of providing a quick one-minute arm workout.

4 Use filtered water
It will make your coffee taste better and avoid impurities from building up on your cafetière or stove-top pot.

5 Don't burn the beans
Always wait for one minute before you pour on the boiled water. This way you'll avoid burning the coffee and giving it a bitter taste.

6 Equipment
If you're using a cafetière (aka French press), allow 10g of coffee for every 160ml of water. Let it steep for five minutes. Grind the coffee coarsely so there's little resistance when you eventually push the plunger down. With a stove-top pot, use a medium grind of coffee and pack it really firmly. Heat it over a low to medium heat. Remove it from the heat as soon as it starts bubbling.

7 Keep equipment clean
Always wash your coffee equipment thoroughly soon after you've used it.

8 Storage tips
Keep your coffee away from sunlight and in an airtight container. Some argue that refrigeration is even better, while others dispute this. Try it out and decide for yourself.

PETROLHEAD'S GARAGE

Petrolheads require the biggest man caves of all. In fact, at the top end, they need an entire car showroom to display their enviable collections. Since that's well beyond the reach of anyone but rock royalty, movie stars, or hedge-fund managers, we'll have to settle for a large garage. One with some very sexy cars in it, however.

So when does a normal garage or car port become an actual motor-car (or motorbike) man cave? It all depends on how often the vehicles get driven. Functional cars may have daily outings, while sports cars and muscle cars are saved for weekend rides out into the country or for days going full throttle at the local racetrack.

Collectors' cars tend to emerge only for special occasions—car rallies, for example, or weddings. Birthdays, at a push. For most of their working lives, classic cars simply get admired, shown off to fellow car enthusiasts, and polished. It's like the difference between a working dog and a pedigree. The former spends its days out in the fields getting dirty and worn out, the latter stays at home, getting brushed and matching the expensive furniture.

Petrolheads can be split between those who simply love cars and bikes and those who like to tinker. Both will happily while away a Sunday afternoon polishing their precious machines, but the latter group are also often found elbow-deep in engine oil, faithfully restoring a classic machine to its former glory. For this they need excellent lighting, a properly stocked tool chest, and a work bench. Real mechanics mount their essential tools on the wall, outlining them with indelible marker pen. The Pirelli calendar hangs proudly nearby.

THE SET UP

- Cars and motorbikes, lots of them
- Workbench
- Tool chest
- Epoxy or tile floor
- Fire extinguisher
- Pirelli calendar

REAL-LIFE PETROLHEAD'S GARAGE

At his Las Vegas mansion, former champion boxer Floyd Mayweather has filled several garages with $15 million (£12 million) worth of sports cars, some of which he never actually drives. Note, however, that this is a man who spends $2,000 (£1,600) a week on haircuts so, in comparison, that can't really be seen as extravagant.

His collection of motors includes a Bentley Mulsanne, a Bugatti Veyron, three Ferraris (458 Italia, 599 GTB Fiorano, Enzo), a McLaren 650S, a Mercedes-Benz SLS AMG, a Lamborghini Aventador, a Porsche 911 Turbo Cabriolet, and a Rolls-Royce Phantom. The insurance premiums! Oh Christ! The insurance premiums!

PIRELLI

Every petrolhead needs at lest one Pirelli calendar on his man-cave wall. Don't argue. It's the law.

These sometimes less than subtle examples of photographic fine art have been shot by luminaries such as Terence Donovan, Norman Parkinson, Herb Ritts, Annie Leibovitz, Mario Testino, Karl Lagerfeld, and Helmut Newton. They date back to 1963 when the first was published. Since then they have been graced by the likes of Sophia Loren, Cindy Crawford, Kate Moss, Penelope Cruz, and Heidi Klum, in various states of motor-themed undress.

HEAVENLY VEHICLES

Just imagine for a second that you are richer than God. Which cars would you polish in your man cave? Here are some of the most expensive cars ever made.

Koenigsegg CCXR Trevita
$4.8 million (£3.9 million)
With its unique diamond weave carbon-fiber finish, only two of these were ever made.

Lamborghini Veneno
$4.5 million (£3.6 million)
Hitting a top speed of 220mph, this Italian stallion was built to celebrate Lambo's 50th anniversary.

W Motors Lykan Hypersport
$3.4 million (£2.7 million)
The huge power of this Lebanese supercar is good, but jewel-encrusted headlights are better. Classy.

Bugatti Veyron by Mansory Vivere
$3.4 million (£2.7 million)
Swiss tuning company Mansory pimped the interior and bodywork of a Veyron in their luxurious style.

Ferrari Pininfarina Sergio
$3 million (£2.4 million)
Named after legendary car designer Sergio Pininfarina, this roadster started off as a concept car before fans demanded a public release.

Pagani Huayra BC
$2.6 million (£2.1 million)
The original Huayra was immense, this 739 brake horsepower version is even better.

Ferrari F60 America
$2.5 million (£2 million)
Ferrari removed the roof for this tweaked F12. It does 0–60 in 3.1 seconds, so hold onto your hats.

Bugatti Chiron
$2.5 million (£2 million)
The world's fastest production car? We'll take it.

Right, stop there! Slam on the brakes. Even God has now run out of cash.

CYCLE CLUB

Just how many bikes is a man allowed to own? According to one expert, the answer is "n + 1," where "n" is the number of bikes a man currently owns.

To house all these gorgeous machines, you must have a cycling man cave—a living, working museum where you can clean, mend, and gaze fondly upon your trusty steeds.

First off, a note about security. Install a high-grade ground anchor to the floor of your man cave so you can lock your bikes up securely. Otherwise, nasty thieves will creep in during the night and steal your loved ones. Just outside your cave will be a jet wash for easy post-ride cleaning.

The walls of your bike cave should be decorated with all sorts of really cool cycling paraphernalia. A collection of 1970s' race jerseys, for example. Or vintage Tour de France cycling caps. Or pre-war Campagnolo groupsets. You'll need space for bike magazines and books, plus a coffee machine for pre- and post-ride caffeine perks. Ideally you'll have sports channels streamed through to a wall-mounted TV, so that you can watch obscure European road races while you grind out the miles on your turbo-trainer. Bikes that you don't ride regularly—your 1951 Bianchi Paris-Roubaix, for example—can be hung by hooks on the wall.

The wearing of Lycra and cycling caps is *de rigueur* in your bike man cave. Inevitably, you will spend more time in here than actually out riding your bikes.

REAL-LIFE CYCLE CLUB

The Wright brothers may have invented the world's first proper airplane, but their first love was bicycles. So much so that, in 1892, they opened a repair and sales shop that later became the Wright Cycle Company. As they moved between various houses in the town of Dayton, Ohio, they would bring the bike shop with them, and spend many happy hours tinkering and inventing. It was a commercial shop but also, in many ways, their man cave. The profits from the shop eventually funded their experiments in aviation.

THE SET UP

- Bikes, lots of them
- Bike racks
- Bike mechanic stand
- Tools
- Track pump
- Ground anchor
- Turbo-trainer
- Books and magazines
- TV
- Coffee machine

HOW TO INSTALL A GROUND ANCHOR

Nothing attracts thieves like a bicycle man cave. To keep your beauties secure you'll need a ground anchor embedded into the floor, plus a seriously chunky security chain and lock. Here's how to install it all properly.

1 Buy the strongest ground anchor, chain, and lock you can afford.

2 Place the ground anchor on the floor and mark where you need to drill the holes.

3 Use a masonry drill bit to make the holes.

4 Place the metal screw anchors (Rawlplugs) in the holes and secure the ground anchor to the floor with the securing bolts. They normally expand to grip the floor as you tighten them.

5 Fit ball bearings in the bolt heads so that thieves can't undo them. Use a hammer and punch to punch them in.

6 Finally, hammer steel covers onto the top of each bolt head.

TURBO TRAINING

In case you're unfamiliar with these devices, a quick note of explanation: turbo-trainers let you ride your bike stationary and indoors—perfect for winter training in northern climes. With most models, you suspend your rear wheel in a frame, and cycle as you normally would, pedaling against resistance that you can increase or decrease. Some trainers use magnets to create resistance, some use fluid, some use air, and in others you remove your back wheel and attach your rear forks to it. There are also devices called rollers, where you don't remove your back wheel and your bike isn't suspended at all. On these you need to balance as you cycle on the rollers.

Come winter time, when it gets dark, wet, and cold, you'll be spending many long hours grinding out the miles on your turbo-trainer.

TURBO TIPS

- Place your turbo-trainer on a smooth, flat surface where you can get a good view of the TV. Let's be honest, long sessions can be boring, and box sets make the time pass more quickly. Otherwise cue up the stereo with lots of inspirational songs.

- You're going to get sweaty, so place a fan in front of you as you ride.

- Have a towel handy, too, to wipe the sweat.

- You're going to need at least a couple of water bottles, depending on your workout time.

- Use a stopwatch to regulate your turbo sessions. A bike computer is even better.

- Always warm up gradually for 10 minutes or so before you start your turbo session.

- Sometimes you'll want to smash out some long interval sessions. For these you need to ride at 70 percent or 80 percent of your maximum heart rate for between 45 minutes and an hour.

- Other times you might want to grind out high-intensity sessions. For example, you might alternate 30-second bursts at full pace with two-minute periods at a slow pace.

- Always warm down at the end of your session.

The most perfect fishing man cave would be perched high on a sea cliff or beside a crystal-clear chalk stream. The perfect hunting man cave would be deep in the woods, or on the edge of a safari park. Back in the real world, though, and you might find your suburban backyard isn't quite what you had in mind.

That doesn't stop you creating the world's finest hunting and fishing man cave, however. Center stage will of course be the monstrous head of the largest beast you have ever had the privilege of dispatching. Smaller kills, cased fish, and photos of your biggest fishing catches will occupy other wall space.

Now for the tools of your trade. For security reasons you're going to need to keep all the serious assault rifles in a gun cabinet but antique rifles deserve pride of place on the wall. Perhaps there's room for an enormous crossbow, too. Fishing rods can be suspended from the roof. A woodburner or log fire will complete the frontiersman effect.

THE SET UP

- Hunting trophies
- Hunting rifles
- Gun cabinet
- Fishing rods
- Cased fish
- Fly cabinet
- Woodburner

HUNTING
LODGE

REAL-LIFE HUNTING LODGE

For the final 35 years of his life, and all throughout his presidency, Theodore Roosevelt lived at his huge house, Sagamore Hill, in Long Island, New York. Of the 22 rooms in all, his favorite was his trophy room where he kept the spoils of his hunting in both the Western states of the USA and Africa. The house is now a museum, with many of Teddy's trophies still displayed on the wooden walls.

Roosevelt has to be one of the biggest legends in hunting. Following his time as president, Roosevelt spent just under a year on safari in Africa, where the scientific expedition he was part of trapped or shot an incredible 11,000 animals, including elephants, lions, leopards, cheetahs, and rhinos.

CALL THAT A ROD?

According to *Guinness World Records*, the longest ever fishing rod measured an incredible 73 feet, 7 inches, that's over 22 meters. It was made out of carbon fiber by the Schweizerischer Fischereiverband, or Swiss Fisheries Association, in 2011. Sadly, members weren't able to net themselves a record-breaking catch with the monster rod.

CARE FOR YOUR TROPHIES

Look after your animal heads and they will age a lot better than you will.

Avoid sunlight and damp

"Keeping mounts away from dampness and out of sunlight will go far in preserving the integrity of the hide, the hair, and the coloring," advises the website Taxidermyhobbyist.com. "Excessive dampness can lead to mould and mildew, while overly hot, dry conditions can desiccate the hide and cause it to crack or split."

No grubby fingers

Steve Barker, at hunting website Gohunt.com, says you should touch your animal trophy as little as possible. "Skin oils will discolor fur or hair. Mounts should be given a frequent gentle dusting, but should not be handled more than absolutely necessary."

Vacuum clean

Every two years or so, carry out a comprehensive clean using the duster brush on a vacuum cleaner. "Be sure not to press down on the hair or fur, as it will push dust deeper into the hide," Barker adds. "Always go with the direction of the coat, whether using a vacuum or feather duster."

No oil

Taxidermist John Bellucci, writing for AfricaHunting.com, says it's crucial you never use oil of any kind to clean horns or antlers. "A clean white towel, dampened with water, is all you need."

Sparkling eyes

Clean the eyes using normal window-cleaning fluid and a small artist's paintbrush.

HUNT IN YOUR OWN HOME

Remember that classic video game *Duck Hunt*? Well, things have moved on quite a bit since then and today's hunting simulators are incredibly sophisticated pieces of kit. With recreations of dream hunting scenarios, it's as close as you can get to going on a hunting trip without leaving your house. Get one.

ANTIQUE SHOTGUNS

You'll need to rob a bank to afford these beautiful weapons. Just don't be tempted to saw off the barrels before you do so.

Fabbri over and under shotgun
$170,000 (£138,000)
Only 20 or so Fabbris are built every year. Apparently, at the factory in Italy, the craftsmen work in total silence. With delivery times of up to five years, that's a lot of silence.

Peter Hofer sidelock shotgun
Price on application
This Austrian manufacturer once spent over 21,000 hours working on a single gun. Just half a dozen or so leave his workshop every year.

Boss over and under shotgun
From $130,000 (£105,000)
To buy a gun from this German brand, established in 1812, you have to order over two years in advance.

Purdey over and under shotgun
From $134,000 (£108,000)
Purdey have been making superb over-and-under shotguns ever since they bought out London gunmaker James Woodward & Sons in 1949.

Holland & Holland Royal over and under shotgun
From $121,000 (£98,000)
With its walnut stock and gold engravings, this gun requires over 900 hours to build.

CASED FISH

Nothing taxes a taxidermist as much as a fish. Our aquatic friends lose their color once they dry out and need to be re-painted. But a lovingly stuffed fish will add a certain class to your man cave.

Stewart Pope, who runs the website casedfish.com, is a world expert on collecting fish taxidermy. He bought his first cased fish at the age of 10, back in 1973, and now owns around 200. Here are his key tips on caring for cased fish.

- "Keep the cases out of direct sunlight. If exposed, any colors will fade quickly. The value of the fish reduces dramatically as it loses that original finish."

- "Do not trust the hanging loops that come with any case. These can rot over the years and give way without warning. Cases with more than one loop, or larger cases should also be supported by a shelf to spread the load."

- "Avoid displaying a fish over a radiator or where there may be large fluctuations in temperature."

WOODWORKING AND DIY CAVE

Men in caves love to work with their hands. That primal urge to build and create goes with the territory. But when you break it down, woodworking and DIY is a rather strange hobby. What is it that makes bashing nails, sawing wood, and drilling holes so popular?

Speak to many DIY enthusiasts and they'll agree that for nearly every job started there will be at least one rage-inducing low point. The moment when a project doesn't go quite to plan, which is usually accompanied by a volley of expletives that'd make most rappers blush. It's at this stage, with head held despairingly in hands, that men question why they even bother with DIY? Luckily, men don't give up easily and will persevere with their project until completion. This leads to that euphoric DIY high, the one where you stand back and proudly admire your creation, basking in the feelings of manliness that wash over you. It's these highs that make woodworking and DIY such addictive hobbies and keep men coming back for more.

In many ways, every man cave starts off life as a DIY man cave, given that you'll have to build a few things to put in it. What should go into the perfect DIY man cave? Any of the following wouldn't go amiss: a huge workbench, a lathe, a vice, lots of power tools, drawers full of screws, bolts, nails, and fixings, plus the obligatory wall-mounted hand tools with their shapes drawn round them in indelible marker (see Petrolhead's garage, page 90). What more does any self-respecting red-blooded male need?

The woodworking and DIY man cave is where you will build beautiful mahogany furniture. It is where you will craft old-fashioned wooden toys for your appreciative children. It's where you will carve out a canoe from a tree trunk. It's where you will whittle an entire chess set with your bare hands. It's where you will sweat, swear, and hammer your thumbs as you unsuccessfully put together a cheap Ikea bookshelf. It is the essence of man in cave form.

THE SET UP

- Workbench
- Lathe
- Vice
- All the power tools
- Enough wood to fill a Canadian forest

REALLY SEXY POWER TOOLS

What is it about power tools that makes a man so... Well, manly? The noise? The electricity? The labor-saving capacity? The ever-present threat of self-amputation?

According to the website Artofmanliness.com, these are the key power tools that all men ought to own. Keep them handy in your man cave. Wear safety equipment and tuck your fingers in at all times. Try your best to limit alcohol consumption before use.

Cordless drill
Drill holes anywhere, fast.

Reciprocating saw
A selection of blades will let you cut through wood, metal, tiles, trees, etc.

Oscillating multi-tool
Sand wood, cut pipes, scrape off paint, cut tiles, remove flooring... This ingenious invention will do it all.

Circular saw
Makes quick work of the thickest sheets of wood.

REAL-LIFE WOODWORKING AND DIY CAVE

East Los Angeles is home to a collective of woodworkers called Offerman Woodshop. Led by actor Nick Offerman (he of *Fargo* and *Parks and Recreation* fame), it's a treasure trove of workbenches, lathes, vices, overflowing tool racks, and sawdust. The various members of the collective specialize in traditional hand-crafted joinery and the salvage of fallen trees.

"We like to carve spoons, chainsaw stumps, plank canoes, keep our chisels sharp with stones, build pinball machines and fine furniture," they explain. "From refined modern designs to enormous Middle Earth masterpieces, we build it all while smiling a lot."

Offerman spends much of his free time working with his hands in this enormous workshop. When he's not acting, he is often seen sporting a tool belt around his midriff.

He is author of the book *Good Clean Fun: Misadventures in Sawdust at Offerman Woodshop*, and has released an instructional DVD called *Fine Woodstrip Canoe Building with Nick Offerman*. It's safe to say this man knows his way round a toolbox.

The workshop members sell their products (and include a couple of women), so it's not strictly a man cave. But thanks to all that sweat and sawdust, it deserves a mention here.

NINE FINGERS LEFT

DIY and injuries go together like a cold beer and a job well done. According to *Forbes*, these are the five most dangerous power tools you'll find in a man cave.

1 Nail guns (37,000 people hospitalized every year in the US)
2 Chainsaws (36,000)
3 Table saws (29,000)
4 Circular saws (10,600)
5 Power drills (5,800)

19th Hole

GOLF CLUB

Unfortunately, the laws of physics prevent us from constructing an entire 18-hole golf course inside a man cave. But that doesn't mean we can't have some sort of indoor shrine to the sport; a golf-themed sanctuary, complete with golf simulator and artificial putting green.

In here you will keep all your clubs, equipment, and clothing, plus some excellent memorabilia such as souvenir tees, impressive score cards, and novelty club-head covers. Install a full-length mirror on one wall so you can analyze your swing.

The *pièce de résistance* is a personal 19th hole fully stocked with all the refreshments you will need after a hard evening's practice.

THE SET UP

- Golf simulator
- Artificial putting green
- Mirror
- 19th hole

GOLF SIMULATORS

There exist as many different styles of golf simulator as there are ways to shank a tee shot. Some simulate a shot as you swing a remote-control device. Others use high-speed cameras, sensor mats, computer software, or laser tracking to monitor the real swing of your real club and the path of your real ball as you hit it into the simulator screen. Most let you virtually play the best golf courses on the planet.

Simulators range from well under the cost of an annual membership at your local golf club to prices that might even make Jordan Spieth think twice. If money is no object, then why not consider the Full Swing Golf S4 Simulator? It's what the pros use to fine-tune their swings. Sure, prices start at an eye-watering $25,000 (£20,000), but for that you get a pixel-perfect recreation of over 80 courses, including The Belfry, Firestone, and Gleneagles. According to the company's website, the system boasts "the ultimate in ball flight technology and accuracy," a playing surface that changes gradient, and levels of customization that were previously unheard of. Want to practice your bunker shots in wet conditions with a westerly wind blowing at 23 miles per hour? You can with this incredible program.

HOW TO BUILD AN INDOOR PUTTING GREEN

Are you considering setting up a putting green in your backyard? Trust us, it's far too much like hard work. Those things need mowing on a daily basis, taking into consideration the direction of the cut and the blade height of your mower. Plus, where's the fun in getting soaked in a rain storm while you trim the edges of the holes by hand with a pair of scissors?

Instead, why not build an artificial green indoors? That way you'll spend many happy hours sinking balls on your man cave putting green and not have to waste any time trying to reseed the bald patches by the 7th hole. The shape and size of your green will depend on the space available, but aim for a minimum area of 4 x 8 feet (1.2 x 2.4 meters). And, whatever you do, don't be tempted to add a windmill.

1 Use four wooden planks to create the rectangular frame for your green. The planks should be deep enough to accommodate golf holes. Connect the boards with strong screws and add L-brackets on the corners to secure them.

2 Attach several cross planks to the inside of your rectangular frame, so that you'll be fully supported when you walk on top of it.

3 Place a thick sheet of plywood on top of your frame, nailing it to the support planks beneath.

4 Use a hole-saw blade to drill holes in the corners of your putting green, ensuring that they're well clear of any cross planks. Don't drill a hole in the middle since it won't give you a long enough putt. Remember that a regulation golf cup has a diameter of $4^1/_4$ inches (10.8 centimeters). Sand off the edges of each hole.

5 Using carpet glue, stick a layer of artificial grass to the plywood, stretching it flat as you progress. Cut off any extra material with a utility knife. To ensure a flat surface, unroll your artificial grass a few days before you glue it, lying it on the floor, using heavy books to keep it flat.

6 Use the utility knife to cut out the holes through the artificial grass. Insert golf cups and flags into the holes. You can buy these online.

7 Finally, give your green a perimeter by nailing large-diameter dowel rods around the outside. Paint them green to match the artificial grass.

THE 19TH HOLE

You've got the simulator set up and have completed the build on your pristine indoor putting green, but don't forget about the social side of golf—the clubhouse bar. This can be anything from a fridge full of beer to a bar stocked with the finest single malts picked up on your pilgrimage to St Andrews. Make sure you've got space for a few comfortable chairs and consider installing a TV. That way you can keep up with the action on the PGA Tour. Whether there's a dress code required to enter your bar is entirely up to you.

STARGAZING OBSERVATORY

Just how serious are you about astronomy? With a generous budget you could spend thousands having a motorized observatory dome built in your backyard. A cheaper option would be an observatory shed with a rolling roof. Both of these will house your telescopes, protect you from the elements, allow you to view in any direction, and, most crucially of all, cut down on light pollution. Highly practical if you live in or near the bright lights of a big city.

If that all sounds a bit too Hubble (and expensive), why not simply locate your astronomy man cave in the attic, observing the stars through the skylight? As long as local light pollution isn't too severe, you'll still get good views of the heavens.

Where you mustn't scrimp is on the telescope. Furnish your home observatory with the finest machine you can afford. If that means forking out on a pro-level catadioptric, then so be it.

Remember to leave room for all the constellation charts and reference books.

THE FINEST ORRERIES

An orrery is a mechanical model of the solar system. There are various versions, depending on which planets are featured— a grand orrery is normally the Sun and all the planets. (Many antique orreries were built before all the planets were discovered, or before poor Pluto was declassified, so there's a good variety of versions out there.) A model of the Earth, Sun, and Moon is called a tellurion; just the Earth and Moon is a lunarium; Jupiter and its many moons is a jovilabe.

Funnily enough, there's not a huge demand for orreries, making it rather tricky/expensive to procure one for your man cave. What with all the flat-screen TVs and laptops, working models of the solar system aren't exactly jumping off the shelves at your local department store. (Criminal, isn't it?) For that reason there are very few professional orrery-makers out there still plying their trade.

One specialist bucking the trend is Australian instrument-maker Brian Greig. Something of a perfectionist, Brian spends between six weeks and six months creating each of his models which now grace observatories, museums, and private houses all over the world. "The executed work must exhort the brain, challenge the eye, and test the hand," he says of his work. Bang on, Brian.

THE SET UP

- Observatory dome or shed
- Telescopes
- Binoculars
- Orrery
- Charts of the night sky and well-stocked reference library
- Plenty of coffee to keep you awake

HOW TO CUT DOWN LIGHT POLLUTION

High up in the mountains, or deep in the wilderness—that's the best place to locate your observatory if you want to avoid light pollution. But most of us live in the real world and, unfortunately, that normally means dealing with a lot of artificial light pollution. Here are some clever ways to reduce its effect.

Find the shadow
If you're building an observatory in the backyard or in your attic, position your telescope well away from the illumination of any nearby street lights.

The right climate
Light pollution occurs when artificial light shines into the sky and is reflected back to Earth by water vapor, dust, and pollution in the sky. Avoid observing the stars during the worst periods, when it's very humid or dry and dusty.

Filter out pollution
You can buy specialist filters for your telescope, which suppress the local light pollution.

Cool shades
Most telescopes come with a lens shade or dew shield, which prevents the build-up of moisture during nighttime observations and cuts down on light pollution. If the latter is particularly bad, you can extend the lens shade using thick, black card.

Cover up
Try covering your head with a dark cloth. This will help your pupils to dilate more, allowing you to see better through the light pollution. If it worked for Victorian photographers, it just might work for you, too.

Keep up with the Joneses
Lovely as your neighbors may be, there's a good chance they're contributing to your local light pollution. To combat this, why not invite them round for a stargazing party and ask them to turn off all their house lights before they come over?

Become a night owl
Towns and cities normally get darker as the night progresses. 3am is a good time to catch those constellations.

HOME DOMES

The dream stargazing man cave is a domed observatory, but unless you're an absolute whiz with a hammer, constructing one at home from scratch is probably beyond the capabilities of your average amateur astronomer. Luckily, there are a number of kits on the market that allow you to build your own observatory with minimal fuss and often for under $3,000 (£2,500). The basic kits come with enough room to fit a 12-inch aperture telescope, which is plenty powerful enough for some serious deep-sky observing. The rotating domes give you a 360° view, but even without moving you can still see half the night sky, perfect for your imaging sessions. These domes are often fully customizable, meaning you can add a motor and solar panels, or create additional storage space for your equipment. They are also designed to be fully waterproof and can be secured to a concrete base with a ground anchor (see page 97), meaning your equipment will be very safe. The main issue you'll have is dragging yourself away from the thing, or trying to stay awake at work following an all-night stargazing session.

THE ULTIMATE OFFICE

If you're lucky enough to work from home, you really ought to transform your office into some sort of nerve center, the kind of place from which a Bond villain might plot world domination. After all, you're going to spend well over a third of your life in here. Desk jockeys must have pedigree desks to ride if they want to win the race.

The location of your home office doesn't really matter, although an inspiring view will help, and the ability to look out of a window will stop your eyes getting too fatigued by the computer. Spend too long in your basement over the winter and you're likely to go stir crazy.

In fact home workers need to take special precautions not to go stir crazy, especially during the colder months when the days shorten. Background music is important, as is air conditioning, the color of your home office walls, office plants, and a ready supply of caffeine. But perhaps most crucial of all is a comfortable desk and chair set-up.

Then just sit back (in underpants and an old T-shirt if necessary—you are your own boss after all) and start plotting world domination.

OFFICE PLANTS

Yearning for a yucca? Craving a cactus? Pining for an indoor conifer? Office plants will improve your man-cave office on many levels. Recent research at Australia's University of Technology Sydney discovered that the presence of plants in working environments reduces anxiety and tension by 37 percent, depression by 58 percent, anger and hostility by 44 percent, and fatigue by 38 percent.

THE SET UP

- Desk
- Ergonomic chair
- Computer, plus ergonomic keyboard and mouse
- Desk light
- Plants
- Sound system
- Telephone headset
- Coffee machine
- Mini fridge
- Notice board

THE ULTIMATE DESK SET UP

First things first, unless you work for some ultra-hip Silicon Valley startup where the company ergonomic experts insist everyone works suspended by a complicated series of wires, every home office requires a desk. Your primary consideration for this is comfort. Yes, you can buy yourself an all-singing, all-dancing work surface made of mahogany, or copper, even platinum, with a white rhino hide-upholstered chair, but if they're not comfortable, they won't do the job. Get your priorities right. After all, this is where you'll be spending most of your working life.

"The U-shaped desk is best," says Matt Perman, author of *How to Set Up Your Desk*. "It gives you more space, and enables you to implement left-to-right workflow. You can have your physical inbox on the left side, move items in front of you to work on them, and place on your right side the stuff you've finished working on."

"You want your desk to be like a cockpit," he adds. "Easy, fingertip access to the things you use most often, and enough surface area to organize your (non-computer) work on the desktop."

Your computer and chair should be adjusted so that your feet are flat on the ground, your knees are bent, your hips are slightly higher than your knees, and your eyes are level with the top of your computer screen.

CONVINCING YOUR EMPLOYER TO LET YOU WORK FROM HOME

For many, the opportunity to work in the comfort of their own home is the ultimate office environment. Just think, no more jam-packed rush-hour trains; at least an extra hour in bed thanks to a commute that can be measured in steps rather than miles; an end to the awkward office conversations as you wait to use the microwave… If you're reading this and wishing it was you sat at your desk in your PJs rather than a stuffy suit, then try the following lines of argument on your boss.

Save money

This is the big one. According to a study at Stanford University, a company will save an average of $2,000 (£1,600) a year by letting an employee work from home.

Reduce stress

Work-related stress is all too common. Thankfully, those who work at home are 25 percent less likely to suffer from this affliction.

Increase productivity

By eliminating the need for long commute times, home workers actually spend more hours at their desk than their office-based counterparts. Furthermore, happier workers tend to work harder and are more willing to work longer hours.

Maintain a better work-life balance

Working from home offers employees a more flexible schedule to the standard nine to five. This improves morale and allows people to spend more time on their interests outside of the office.

Be healthier

Without constant access to calorific snacks and fatty lunchtime takeouts, workers can maintain a healthier diet at home. This leads to fewer illnesses and days off sick.

SIT DOWN IN STYLE
Xten ergonomic chair
$2,495 (£2,000)

This is where the world's most pampered behinds deserve to sit. The Xten ergonomic office chair was created—at an alleged cost of $1.5 million (£1.2 million)—by the good people at Italian company Pininfarina who spend much of their time designing for the likes of Ferrari and Maserati. What's so special about their chairs then? First off, there's the gel seating that "forms to the contour of the body and reduces seating pressure and fatigue." Then there's the adjustable lumbar support, headrest, and armrest. Finally, both the seat and the back of the chair tilt independently of each other. If you can ever bring yourself to stop fiddling with it, you might actually get some work done.

THE WORLD'S MOST EXPENSIVE DESK
Parnian desk
$200,000 (£160,000)

If you've got money to burn, and the butler to burn it for you, then you might want to consider making this your desk of choice. Short of commissioning a custom-made work surface in diamond-encrusted solid gold, this may well be the most expensive desk ever made. Designed by American furniture specialist Parnian, it graces the reception at the company's headquarters in Scottsdale, Arizona, and features six types of exotic wood, including ebony and Carpathian elm. "The inlays and burls used along with the perfection of the signature Parnian finish lets people know that the person sitting behind that desk has truly made it," claim the manufacturers. And they should know, since they truly made it.

REAL-LIFE ULTIMATE OFFICE

Matthew Weiner is the award-winning screenwriter and creator of TV series *Mad Men*. Like the characters that populate his story of 1960s' advertising executives, he knows all about cool interiors. In fact, his home office, in Los Angeles, is so cool it squeaks.

With huge glass windows on all four sides, and views of the garden, the swimming pool, and the Californian foothills in the distance, it's something of a fishbowl. Except of course there are no neighbors overlooking him.

"It's kind of like being outside," Weiner told *House Beautiful* magazine. "At night it has an orange-ish glow that illuminates the yard; really beautiful."

At one end of the rectangular structure is a floor-to-ceiling open-backed bookshelf stocking Weiner's myriad awards and the poetry, short stories, and plays that most inspire him. Then there's an old-school black leather executive chair and antique wooden desk facing toward the opposite end of the room where he has installed sofas and a coffee table. Roman blinds and an ornate triple light shade hang from the ceiling.

"The light is what I like most about working in here. I need a good dose of light. That's partly why I've flourished in Los Angeles. It ignites my creativity. I'm not going to lie, I've spent time just watching dust particles float in the air, but even on a cloudy day, it's bright in here. You cannot be sad in this room."

WALL COLOR

When it comes to decorating your home office, you'll have photos, pictures, and notice boards on your man-cave office walls. But what color paint job should you opt for?

"White doesn't help us be productive, and most work environments are white, off-white, or gray," says Nancy Kwallek from the University of Texas School of Architecture.

Much better to choose a bold color. Blue is relaxing and calming, and encourages clear thought. Red promotes passion and excitement. It's a great boost for people who work with their hands. Green reduces stress. Yellow is associated with fun and happiness, but too much can cause you to lose your temper.

THE 20-20-20 RULE

Staring at a computer screen all day really is bad news. Down that path lie headaches, eye strain, and eventual brain death. To give your eyes a break, ideally you need a window to look out of, but what else can you do to stop the optical rot?

The best thing to help your straining eyes is to remember what's known as the 20-20-20 rule. Every 20 minutes you should spend 20 seconds looking at something 20 feet out of your window. Whether that's a tree, your lawnmower, or the neighbor's wife taking a shower doesn't really matter. It's all about something called accommodation—in other words, when your eye muscles change focus from close-up to distance.

There's no getting round it: pet houses smell. You can't locate them in the spare bedroom for risk of stinking out the house with rabbit poop or guano. The garden shed is best, unless you plan on keeping tropical animals, in which case you'll need to ensure your loved ones are warm in winter. The basement could make for a great serpentarium.

The best pet houses are those that represent all the major animal groups, but without risk of predation. A zoo, in other words. So, in one corner we have docile mammals, such as rabbits and guinea pigs. In the other, aggressive reptiles, such as snakes and lizards. Then parrots in large cages with adjoining perches, and a huge aquarium across one wall. Feel free to stick the stick insects anywhere you like.

PET HOUSE

THE SET UP

- Rabbit hutch
- Parrot cage and perch
- Vivarium, terrarium, and serpentarium
- Aquarium

REAL-LIFE PET HOUSE

American publishing mogul William Randolph Hearst was a keen animal lover, so when he began building the incredible Hearst Castle in 1919, at the time the most expensive private home in the United States, it made sense for him to add a man cave where he could keep a few pets. Well, man cave might be doing a disservice to Animal Hill, the private zoo where Hearst kept animals including monkeys, orang-utans, camels, ostriches, kangaroos, leopards, lions, tigers, and even an elephant. Following a period of financial instability in the 1930s, Hearst was forced to begin dismantling the zoo, but zebras still roam the grounds of the castle, which is now a California state park.

PET SCHOOL

As a responsible owner of your pet house, you're going to want to do some basic animal training. Having said that, it does depend on your menagerie, because you might be there for a while if you try to train a goldfish—the three-second memory makes for slow progress. If you are going to put the hours in, don't limit your training to tricks, instead get the animals to do something useful. Any pet could do a lot worse than follow the example of Zac the Macaw. This California-based bird can crack open 35 drinks cans in a minute, the perfect barman for parties.

JAW-DROPPING ANIMALS

Dogs and cats make cute pets, but you want the visitors who come to your pet house man cave to be in awe of your collection. You want to make them feel like they're actually in a zoo. Wow them with these exotic pets.

Tarantula

Eight legs, two sharp fangs, and a guaranteed emotional reaction from all your friends. These hairy arachnids can grow to the size of a dinner plate.

Emperor scorpion

Armed with just a mild venom, emperor scorpions are docile enough to make suitable pets. Watch out for the big claws, however.

Burmese python

Cool, calm, and very sinister, these bad boys can grow up to 13 feet (4 meters) in length. Don't leave them unattended with the mice.

Boa constrictor

Not surprisingly, they like a good cuddle.

Giant African land snail

They don't do much but they're surprisingly graceful and can grow up to 8 inches (20 centimeters) long.

Giant land crab

A quick way to get rid of your kitchen scraps.

Chameleon

Those weird eyes, that interminable tongue, the skin that changes color—there's always something going on with a chameleon.

Poison dart frogs

Anyone who's tuned into a David Attenborough documentary will know about these lethal, brightly colored frogs, whose skin is so toxic they can take a man out just by touching its skin. Luckily, those bred in captivity aren't poisonous, but the visitors to your cave don't have to know that.

LOOKING AFTER LIZARDS

Some of the most impressive animals to have in your pet house will be your collection of reptiles. If you've not had a lizard before, here are a few things you need to consider in order to keep your new pets healthy.

Pick the right animal

Leopard geckos, blue-tongued skinks, and bearded dragons are good starter lizards because they are quite happy to be handled. Others, such as chameleons and iguanas are better for those with prior experience of lizard ownership.

Choose the right cage

Make sure you get a cage, also known as a vivarium or terrarium, that's big enough for your pet—leopard geckos don't need a lot of space, but bearded dragons and skinks require a good-sized tank. It should be fully secure, so there is zero chance of any escape attempts. Look out for cages that retain heat, because they'll help with your electricity bills.

Heat it up

Reptiles are cold blooded, therefore you're going to have to provide them with a range of temperatures—known as the thermal gradient—so that they can regulate their body heat. A heat lamp at one end of the cage will replicate the basking temperature of their natural habitat—for many lizards this will be around 90–100°F (32–38°C), but be certain to check this with the seller. They will also require a sheltered spot in the cage that's around 20°F (10°C) cooler. Get a thermometer to make sure the temperature is optimal.

Let there be light

As well as the heat lamp, you'll need to provide your lizard with ultraviolet light—specifically UVA and UVB—so that it can produce the necessary vitamins for survival. These will need to be switched off at night to replicate the natural 24-hour light-and-dark cycle.

Hot and humid

Depending on your chosen breed, you might be required to create a humid environment within the cage. This can be done easily with a few sprays of water from a mister. Invest in a hygrometer to monitor air humidity.

Food and drink

A constant supply of water is essential and should be changed daily. Some lizards are happy to drink from a bottle, while others prefer bowls, and some even enjoy bathing. Foodwise, most lizards are carnivores and a varied diet of insects, preferably live ones, is best. Omnivore lizards can be given fruit and vegetables as well.

The lizard lounge

Reptiles like a place to shelter away from prying eyes. Two hiding places are best—one close to the heat lamp and one in a cool spot. A few rocks to bask on will make a good addition, as will some driftwood or branches, particularly if your lizard likes to climb. Vines, ferns, and tropical mosses add interest, but live plants will need additional care, so perhaps look at fake instead. On the floor of your cage, adding reptile bark or Astroturf can work well. Don't use printed newspaper as lizards can eat this.

Cleaning

Be prepared to clean the cage on a weekly basis, and regularly remove any uneaten food.

REAL-LIFE PET HOUSE

While you might be OK with tanks packed with goldfish you won at the fair, the best man-cave aquariums really should include a few species that are a little less common. Be warned, these fish don't come cheap, particularly if you want to get hold of a Platinum Arowana, the world's rarest and most expensive fish. The cost? A cool $400,000 (£325,000).

NUCLEAR
BUNKER

Back during the Cold War, a nuclear fallout shelter in your basement, or deep beneath your backyard was seen as a sensible precaution against highly likely Armageddon. Fortunately, frosty relations between the superpowers have long since thawed and, nowadays, a nuclear shelter is more of a museum than a practical sanctuary from all-out atomic destruction.

Saying that, you can never be too prudent. What if Islamic State got hold of a dirty bomb? What if the North Koreans lose their collective short temper once and for all? What if Putin or Trump's finger "accidentally" slips on the big red button? Sure, your friends might call you paranoid, but better safe than sorry, eh?

For obvious reasons, your nuclear shelter needs to be underground. A flimsy garden shed or an elevated loft space won't protect you from the ravages of a radioactive thermal blast. Should you decide to build it beneath your backyard, you'll need at least a meter of soil between you and ground level. Inside you should stock supplies to last you for a minimum of two weeks.

CHOOSING MATERIALS

Let's face it, in the event of a nuclear explosion your standard brick or timber-framed house is going to crumble quicker than Tiger Woods's golfing career. Instead you've got to look at materials that are going to offer a decent amount of protection from those errant radiation particles. The absolute daddy of the shielding world is lead, and you'd need walls that are 4 inches (10 centimeters) thick to protect you from lethal gamma rays. Next is steel, which requires a thickness of 10 inches (25 centimeters), followed by concrete at 24 inches (60 centimeters). The most cost-effective method is regular soil or sand. If you surround your shelter with 3 feet (1 meter) of packed soil—sandbags or earthbags will do—you should survive.

THE SET UP

- Battery-powered radio
- At least two weeks' supply of tinned food
- At least two weeks' supply of water
- Oil lamp and candles
- Torch and batteries
- Portable stove
- Matches
- Camping toilet
- First-aid kit
- Kearny air pump
- Kearny fallout meter

GOURMET NON-PERISHABLES

Just because nuclear Armageddon has occurred, that's no reason to let living standards slip. While armies destroy each other up above, you could be dining on the finest tinned or bottled food and drink known to man.

Foie gras

After weeks in your fallout shelter, you certainly won't need to be force-fed to dine on this French culinary delicacy. Unlike the poor geese who provided it.

Caviar

Russians treasure this stuff almost as much as they adore their nuclear arsenal. Aged for 20 years and packaged in a 24-carat gold case, this is considered the most expensive caviar on the planet. $25,000 (£20,000) a pop.

White truffles

It takes a very well-trained pig to locate these Italian tubers, which are harvested in the fall. Should nuclear war occur at any other time of year, you can always opt for truffles in a jar.

Stilton

This classic English cheese will last for months in the dark of your nuclear shelter, although its pungent smell might force you out of the shelter before you intended to. One brand, Clawson, even once produced a gold-leaf version that cost around $70 (£60) a slice.

Champagne

If nuclear war could produce a winner (theoretically impossible), this is what they might toast victory with. It's a single bottle of Champagne called Gout de Diamants that retails for $1.5 million (£1.2 million). That's mainly thanks to the solid-gold label, and the embedded 19-carat diamond.

PIMP YOUR NUCLEAR CRIB

You've completed your bunker and you're just about ready for the bombs to start raining down, but what are you going to put in there? For a family of four, the minimum you're going to need are two bunk beds for sleeping, a water supply, food, and a bucket to use for the bathroom. However, since you're going to be down there for a while you might as well channel your inner interior designer and make it look homely.

Firstly, start with a few pictures to decorate the walls—maybe some beautiful landscapes to remind you of the world that won't be there when you crawl out the shelter and find everything's turned to dust. No one likes the idea of having to go to the toilet in front of their nearest and dearest, so spare your blushes by screening off a composting toilet close to the entrance to the bunker. A decorative toilet-roll cover and vase of fake flowers will pretty up this space.

Next, a little kitchen area is a worthy addition to any shelter and will allow you to cook up a storm with those tins of baked beans or boxes of cereal (for more ideas, see above). Just remember to stock up before Armageddon hits—Whole Foods will probably close early in the event of a nuke attack.

Finally, you don't want to be lying in your bunk all day—a table and set of camping chairs will make things so much more civilized. A small library with a few well-chosen books will help pass the time. Perhaps post-apocalyptic classics like Cormac McCarthy's *The Road* or *Alas, Babylon* by Pat Frank would make good additions?

INDEX

ACKNOWLEDGMENTS

Thanks to the following cavemen who helped with research: Charles Howgego (Home Brewery),
Matt Tasker (Music Man Cave and Stargazing Observatory), Ian Neil (Nightclub), John Aparicio
(Photography Studio), George Laguillo (Foodie Kitchen and Home Gym), Jeremy Bliss (Wine Cellar),
Gideon Knowles (Train Set and Modeling Cave), and Pete Jorgensen (pretty much all the man caves).
Thanks also to Eoghan O'Brien for the design and John Riordan for the brilliant illustrations.